ALBERT CAPELLANI

ALBERT CAPELLANI

PIONEER OF THE SILENT SCREEN

CHRISTINE LETEUX

FOREWORD BY KEVIN BROWNLOW

UNIVERSITY PRESS OF KENTUCKY

Editorial and Sales Offices: The University Press of Kentucky
663 South Limestone Street, Lexington, Kentucky 40508-4008
www.kentuckypress.com

Cataloging-in-Publication data is available from the Library of Congress.

ISBN 978-0-8131-6643-8 (hardcover : alk. paper)
ISBN 978-0-8131-6644-5 (epub)
ISBN 978-0-8131-6645-2 (pdf)

This book is printed on acid-free paper meeting
the requirements of the American National Standard
for Permanence in Paper for Printed Library Materials.
♾

Manufactured in the United States of America.

Member of the Association of
American University Presses

Contents

Photographs follow page 64

Foreword

Kevin Brownlow

It is staggering to think that Albert Capellani's *La Glu* (1913), made so superbly and acted so naturalistically, was put out a few months before D. W. Griffith had released his first four-reeler into the Stone Age of the American feature.

Capellani, a genial, red-haired, well-upholstered man, with the sort of beard worn by Impressionist painters, was one of the shining lights of the early cinema. It is baffling that it has taken so long for his films to be made available. I first encountered his work in Germany in the 1970s, when I saw a battered copy of *Camille* (1916), of such dim quality it was hard to make out which actress was playing the lead. A recent restoration from the Czech archives makes all the difference: it was Clara Kimball Young.

Working on a television series a few years later, I went to Hollywood to view films from the MGM vaults. I had requested King Vidor's *La Bohème* (1926). I received Capellani's *La Vie de Bohème* (1916), a film I didn't think existed. I remember being thrilled by the photographic quality—right off the camera negative—and equally impressed by the way it was made. Even the art direction, by Frenchman Ben Carré, was exceptional. Carré was still alive in those days, and I telephoned to congratulate him. "The art direction is much better than in the King Vidor version," I said. In his heavily accented French, he replied, "I did that as well." Carré remembered Capellani as "a good colleague," a man who, unlike some in Hollywood, knew the classics and would never have done anything to cheapen them.

A hundred years ago, before audiences grew familiar with film technique, directors felt it sensible to cover each scene in a single shot; this equivalent of the view from the stalls aroused no objections except from progressive filmmakers. They felt it absurd that audiences should object to the moving camera ("makes us feel seasick") or to a close-up of an actor ("where's the rest of him?").

Capellani straddled the two points of view—the primitive era, when film language barely existed; and the experimental era, when attempts were made to give film a personality distinct from the theater.

One American critic felt that Capellani told his version of *Germinal* even more effectively than Zola himself: "The skill of the adapter and director is beyond all praise. . . . *Germinal* is several thousand miles away from the conventional melodrama. It vibrates with the real life all around us. . . . It is in the true sense of the word a masterpiece" (*Moving Picture World,* January 24, 1914).

A headline in *Photoplay* magazine in January 1917 described Capellani as "A Sweet-Tempered Director." Any director who can finish an eight-reel picture and still be on speaking terms with his players, property man, or wife, they said, deserved such a description.

I revere Capellani as one of those French directors, like Maurice Tourneur, who came to the United States as if to show the Americans how to do it. I have a fantasy that French film companies with branches in America would each month survey the work of their American counterparts. All too often—and this is imagination, mind—a collective groan would be heard and the imprecation "*Ah, non, les Americains!*" Eventually, it was decided to send a handful of their best directors to improve the Americans by example. The results support this hypothesis. Tourneur brought a standard of beauty beyond anything the Americans had seen. Capellani taught them how to produce historical films, epics, and sophisticated romances, and to make them with intelligence, humor, and sagacity.

Louis Gasnier was another French director whose high reputation led him to America. But his films have not stood the test of time, whereas Capellani stands as a true artist, with a body of work second to none. As Mariann Lewinsky writes, "He had tremendous feeling for sets and costumes, for special effects, for stories with a backstage setting and for stars. He worked with Mistinguett, Napierkowska and Nazimova; and under Capellani's direction stage stars became film stars" (*Il Cinema Ritrovato*, 24th ed., 2010).

In the mid-twenties, when Abel Gance was unable to secure the associate directors he wanted for *Napoléon* (1927), he asked for Capellani. History doesn't relate what happened to prevent this, but to be asked to codirect that remarkable picture is an indication of how highly the man was regarded. Gance also planned that Capellani's great actor Henry-Krauss should occupy a prominent role in the film.

In 2010 and 2011, Bologna presented a two-part retrospective of Capellani, and we found ourselves queuing up for epics like *Les Misérables* (1912), of unprecedented length (over two hours), and to our surprise being totally absorbed. Yes, the films were handled in master shot, but Capellani proved that if you can stage a scene with authority and conviction, it doesn't matter how slender your coverage.

In this book you will read as much as is known about this remarkable artist. Christine Leteux has researched original documents and has discovered that much of what was written about the man was thoroughly misleading. So now we have the films—and now we have the facts. There is no further excuse to neglect this inspired pioneer.

Introduction

My first encounter with Albert Capellani's work dates from May 2010. I had gone to Forum des Images, a Parisian film library offering a good selection of silent French films. I had chosen a few appealing titles among those available on video and proceeded to watch *Notre-Dame de Paris* (1911), which proved a real downer, a perfect museum piece. The painted backdrops, flat lighting without depth, and overacting of the performers were a complete disappointment. I could have stopped there and not researched this filmmaker any further. However, curiosity prevailed, and I went back to see *Les Misérables* (1912). In spite of a particularly grainy print, I loved this adaptation of Victor Hugo's novel—and I noticed a young Mistinguett playing Eponine. But what made me decide that Capellani was a great filmmaker was the discovery of his masterpiece, *Germinal* (1913). I was flabbergasted at the intelligence of the performers, especially Sylvie and Henry-Krauss, and by the emotional intensity of the film.[1] Yet I discovered it in rather unfavorable circumstances, as a low-resolution video on the Gaumont-Pathé archives website. In spite of it, Sylvie's Catherine Maheu managed to capture my attention, as did Henry-Krauss's marvelous Etienne Lantier.

At this stage, I knew virtually nothing about Albert Capellani. I had only seen a picture of him on the Internet and learned he had a beard and pale blue eyes. The successive release of the Pathé DVD box with four feature films and of the Bologna Festival DVD allowed me to discover more works of Capellani. I became a fan, as I was of other filmmakers of the teens, such as Léonce Perret, the Russian Evgeny Bauer, and the Swedes Victor Sjöström and Mauritz Stiller.

This book was born of my encounter with Robert de Laroche. I was looking for a publisher for a Kevin Brownlow book I wanted to translate. As we were talking, he suggested I write a biography of Albert Capellani. At first, I had doubts. How could I gather enough information in such a short time? After spending a week researching the subject, I realized it was doable. In addition, the research looked exciting. I then met Bernard Basset-Capellani, Capellani's grandson, who proved inexhaustible on the subject. He had a passionate interest in his grandfather's life and work. I was already fascinated by Capellani's work, and I was soon captivated by his life.

The scattered information published about Albert Capellani proved unreliable, if not completely wrong. I realized quickly I would have to start from scratch and follow methodically the thread of his life to establish properly his career. I had to research all the traces a person can leave behind, such as birth and death certificates, marriage license, military records, and census or electoral registers.

After several months, I managed to work out more precisely Capellani's life. Yet, how difficult it was! Here is a pioneer filmmaker who left virtually no written traces. The archives that should have contained handwritten papers were empty. Even his own family has no letters. It was only after a quest of several months that I managed to find two handwritten letters by Capellani. By a strange coincidence, they were kept just a few yards away from his place of birth. I was in the Maison de Victor Hugo Museum, Place des Vosges, where I photographed those precious relics. When I left, I went on a pilgrimage to 27 Boulevard Beaumarchais, the place where Albert Capellani was born on August 23, 1874. After turning left around the well-named Café Victor Hugo, I walked on the deliciously evocative Rue du Pas de la Mule. Once I arrived at the crossing with Boulevard Beaumarchais, I stopped in front of number 27. There was no plaque mentioning Capellani's birth. But the building, with a music shop on the ground floor, was being refurbished by the local authorities and would be converted into council housing. In this area of Paris, nowadays so gentrified, this renovation seemed to remind us of its past, when it was a working-class district.

Introduction

I now invite you to follow me in the footsteps of Albert Capellani. May this book give him a second life and remove him for good from the dungeon of film history.

1

From the Marais to the Batignolles

Albert Capellani's father was a Parisian by adoption. Charles Capellani was born in Thoirette in the mountainous department of Jura in eastern France on August 9, 1845. Charles lost his father at an early age and thereafter lived with his mother—who had independent means—in the 14th arrondissement of Paris, on the Left Bank. On October 28, 1873, he married Valérie-Anna Lévy in front of the registrar of the 3rd arrondissement town hall. Valérie-Anna was only twenty and came with her father and mother to the ceremony. The wedding was performed without a marriage contract, with the consent of all the parents, which suggests that the young couple married for love.

On August 23 of the following year, Charles and Valérie-Anna's first child was born at 27 Boulevard Beaumarchais, in the 4th arrondissement. Albert Lucien was born at one o'clock that morning at his parents' residence. Charles officially registered his son's birth two days later, listing his and his wife's occupations as employee and seamstress. Albert inherited his mother's blue eyes, and he had blond hair. Being from different religions—Charles was a Catholic while Valérie-Anna was Jewish—the parents decided not to give any religious education to their children, probably in order to leave them free to choose their own faith.

On the ground floor of the building at 27 Boulevard Beaumarchais was a manufacturer of stringed instruments managed by Hippolyte Beuscher. (The Paul Beuscher music shop is still located there.) At that time, the area called Le Marais (the Marshland) was a working-class district with a mixed population from various origins. Victor Hugo lived in the Hôtel de Rohan-Guéménée, in the nearby Place des Vosges, from 1832 until 1848. It is still possible nowadays to walk in the Paris streets as Hugo knew them. The Capellani family was not rich. The various family members were employees, typographers, or teachers. They belonged to an educated middle class and were going to give their children every chance to succeed in life thanks to a good education. Albert's parents were obviously extremely open-minded for the time, allowing at least one of their sons to work in entertainment at a time when the self-righteous considered anybody working in show business depraved.

Three years later, Valérie-Anna gave birth to a second son, Paul Henri, on September 2, 1877. He had gray-blue eyes and brown hair. The future star of the Paris stage seemed to be a happy child, but more restless than his elder brother. Some years later, during a little celebration Charles had organized for his and Valérie-Anna's wedding anniversary on October 28, the children gave their mother some flowers, and nine-year-old Paul wrote some verses:

Albert says I'm naughty, mummy,
And I fear it's all too true.
Since everyone repeats the story
I bow my head—what else to do?

But Albert is my older brother,
I must follow, should he lead.
Since he vows his faults to smother
I will be a lamb indeed.

Why should I not promise? Truly,
All our little frets and fights

Could be stilled if we unruly
Children put ourselves to rights:

If we were only *well behaved*
How you would marvel, seeing this:
Our homework done, our lessons learned,
"Sweet dreams!" with a maternal kiss.[1]

The family left the Marais district at the beginning of the 1880s, probably because of Charles's work. In 1884, they migrated to the east of Paris, at 47 Rue des Batignolles in the 17th arrondissement. Marcelle Léontine, the family's first daughter and third child, was born there on August 2, 1884. The little girl did not live long. Infant mortality was still relatively high in those days. Typhoid or scarlet fever often killed the youngest. Marcelle's cause of death is unknown, but she died on April 6, 1889, aged four and a half. One can imagine the parents' grief as they delegated some friends to register the death officially. At the time of their daughter's death they were still living in the Batignolles district, at 35 Rue Brochant.

Emile Zola lived in this area of Paris in the 1860s, in the nearby Rue Truffaut. When he left his home, he would often observe the laundresses in the washhouse across the street. This is how he researched the life of the heroine of *L'Assommoir*. It is noteworthy that as a boy Capellani lived in two districts that were also the homes of Zola and Hugo, both authors he would later adapt to the screen. The Paris of the 1880s was still very close in atmosphere to the one of Zola. Albert as a child thus also knew Zola's working-class Paris with its multitude of craftsmen and was able therefore to re-create it accurately on the screen.

Albert was now old enough to join the small section of the prestigious Lycée Condorcet. During the school year 1885–1886, he got very good grades at math and at drawing. At the time, another future filmmaker was also a pupil at Condorcet. Born Maurice Félix Thomas on February 2, 1876, he would become famous under the name of Maurice Tourneur.[2] Being younger than Albert, he was only in his fifth year of primary school, and he was a good pupil. We do not know if the children knew each other; but they would meet again on the other side of the Atlantic in 1915. Paul joined his brother at Condorcet; unlike Albert, however, in 1887–1888 he was considered a lazy pupil who never learned his lessons.

Albert's father seemed to be earning a good living. In 1889, he was chief clerk in a bank called Comptoir d'Escompte de Paris. This bank clerk had a number of hobbies. He wrote songs and had also patented a new invention called an "Aéroscope," which was intended to give the illusion of traveling into the air with various painted backdrops. He also wanted to offer the best education possible to his two sons. Paul showed an early interest in the arts, and his parents seemed to encourage him. We do not know what Albert's chief interests were at the time. It's quite possible he shared his younger brother's interest in literature and the arts.

Paul and Albert later left Condorcet for Lycée Charlemagne, in the Marais district, for a short period. Then their father decided to send them to a prestigious college where Gustave Eiffel, Jean Jaurès, Léon Gaumont, and Alfred Dreyfus had studied. Paul and Albert joined the Collège Sainte-Barbe, near the Panthéon, in the Latin Quarter. In a letter to the director, Charles Capellani wrote that "he wants his son [Albert] to prepare his baccalaureate in sciences." As for Paul, his parents would like to see him study medicine. His grades had improved a lot since Condorcet. He showed a precocious talent in sculpture. Aged only fifteen, one of his works was even selected for the Salon des Artistes Français. In his fifth year of secondary school, one of Paul's teachers said, "Capellani will do well in his sixth year if he gives himself completely to the very serious studies awaiting him and doesn't get distracted by some artistic concerns, which must remain foreign to him until he has received his full baccalaureate."

In May 1889, shortly after Marcelle's death, the whole family moved to Vincennes, a suburban town east of Paris. Again the move must have had to do with the father's job transfer to a new location. Charles must have obtained a promotion within the Comptoir d'Escompte de Paris. In those days, Vincennes belonged to the Seine department—that is, the same department as Paris. The family lived first at 30 bis, Rue des Carrières. In 1890, Valérie-Anna gave birth to a third son, Charles. Six years later, the child died. This new tragedy hit the family hard. Paul, who was in his final year, failed his baccalaureate in literature. He returned to college for another term before leaving for good. In 1897, he joined the Paris conservatory to study drama.

As for Albert, he successfully entered his final year in Collège Sainte-Barbe. His grades were excellent, as befits a serious and disciplined pupil. Documents are missing, however, to ascertain whether he received his baccalaureate. In 1891, the Vincennes census shows that Albert was still at college. In 1892, aged eighteen, his military record shows he was working as an accountant. He must have followed his father's footsteps into Charles's bank, the Comptoir d'Escompte de Paris. Unfortunately, in those days, military service was compulsory for boys and lasted three years. Rather than waiting to be called up, Albert decided to enlist. On March 27, 1893, he signed up for three years as a volunteer, joining the 45th infantry regiment two days later.

Albert did not show any real interest in a military career. Appointed corporal on September 30, 1893, he asked to become a private again on March 18, 1894, in order to join the geographical department of the 8th Brigade. He then moved to various secretarial jobs in the headquarters and recruitment section. He was back to active service in 1895 and was part of the 2nd expeditionary force sent to Madagascar on April 6, 1895. Back in France in November 6, 1895, he was promoted again to the rank of corporal on November 12. He was at last released from his military duties on March 27, 1896, and became a reservist.

Albert Capellani was now twenty-two. He was five feet, seven inches tall, with blond hair and blue eyes. He was living in Vincennes, at 11 Rue Diderot. Motion pictures had just been born. He could have had little idea that one day he would be employed by the Pathé company, which had just opened in Rue du Polygone. Back in civilian life, he returned to his former job, accounting.

2

From Vincennes
to the Alhambra

In 1896, the Capellanis were living at 11 Rue Diderot in Vincennes. While Albert was away in the army, another brother, Maurice Albert, was born on February 22, 1894. He was twenty years younger than Albert. After the successive deaths of Marcelle and Charles, one can imagine that his mother must have been overprotective, particularly as Paul and Albert were both adults when Maurice was born. After his military service, Albert worked in the same bank as his father, who was now head of the division. Meanwhile Paul joined the National Conservatory of Music on October 23, 1897, to study drama with the great theater actor Charles Le Bargy. As a pupil, he was allowed an exemption from military service for a year. He would nevertheless have to do his service like his brother. A year later, on November 14, 1898, Paul enlisted. He obtained a temporary leave of absence on September 20, 1899, presenting a certificate from the prestigious School of Oriental Living Languages (now the National Institute of Oriental Languages and Civilizations). Was he really a pupil in this school? We can have some doubts, as Paul's chief interest was in theater. We may assume that he obtained that certificate in order to be able to go back to the conservatory. His return to the conservatory is confirmed in the 1900 Vincennes electoral register, where Paul is listed as a pupil there.

In any case, his leave of absence from his military service allowed Paul to finish his studies. On June 21, 1901, he was among the pupils allowed to compete for the final exam in the tragedy and comedy sections as a student of Charles Le Bargy. Among the other competitors, several actors would work later for Pathé under the direction of his brother: Mlle. Sylvie was in Mr. Sylvain's class, and Claude Garry was in Maurice de Féraudy's.[1] A fearless Paul presented for the tragedy section Shakespeare's *Hamlet,* and for the comedy, the part of Perdican in Alfred de Musset's *No Trifling with Love.* On a side note, Sylvie at this time was as removed as possible from her future parts of tragic and frightening elderly women. She presented the part of Rosine in Beaumarchais' *The Barber of Seville* in the comedy section. On July 24, at nine a.m., the pupils faced the jury. Paul obtained an honorable mention *(premier accessit)* in tragedy and comedy, but no prize. The critic from the newspaper *Le Petit Parisien* who recounted the results complained, "The tragedy section was rather dull, as is often the case."[2]

Paul had no time to start a career on the stage. On October 28, 1901, he had to rejoin the army for two years. On October 19, 1903, he was back in civilian life, having attained the rank of corporal, like his brother Albert.

While Paul was in the military, the family suffered a tragic event. In September 1902, their father, Charles, died at the age of fifty-seven. He must have been ill for a while, as the Vincennes census of 1901 indicated he was unemployed. Albert must therefore have had to support the family, including his mother and his younger brother, who was then aged eight. At that time, Albert was employed by the Comptoir Municipal d'Escompte, the bank where his father used to work. The situation must have been difficult, as he had recently gotten married. On November 9, 1901, Albert had married Léonie-Marie Cadé, a very pretty blonde girl aged twenty-five.

Between the years 1903 and 1907, Albert Capellani did not live in Vincennes. His name disappeared from the census and electoral registers. At first, he must have been still working for the Comptoir d'Escompte. However, during this period, his career took a decisive turn. The bank clerk became the administrator of an important Paris music hall, the Alhambra.

The whole family must have tried to stay close together following the father's death. All the addresses I found for the various family members for the period 1903–1907 are situated in the 11th arrondissement, which happens to correspond with the Alhambra. In 1904, Paul was living at 66 Avenue de la République with his mother and his little brother Maurice, who was attending the Lycée Voltaire, at 101 Avenue de la République, from 1904 until 1907.

As for Albert, we can locate him precisely on January 31, 1905, at 38 Boulevard Voltaire (11th arrondissement) when his first child, Roger, was born. By a happy coincidence, Albert's residence was very close to the Alhambra on 50 Rue de Malte. In any case, we have irrefutable confirmation that he was indeed the Alhambra administrator in 1905, thanks to a Nadar portrait dated November 1, 1905.[3]

How did the bank clerk become the Alhambra administrator? This sudden change remains a mystery. However, several interesting leads provide some explanations for Albert's career change. First, there is the Alhambra history. Until the end of 1903, it was called *Théâtre du château d'eau*. Its director was Victor Sylvestre and its administrator H. Legrand. The programs were essentially operettas, such as Hervé's *Mam'zelle Nitouche* or Offenbach's *La Fille du Tambour-Major*. By the end of 1903, a British entrepreneur, Thomas Barrasford, purchased the theater and renamed it L'Alhambra. It reopened in February 1904 with a very different program. No more French operettas. Barrasford managed numerous music halls in Great Britain, including the Lyceum and the Britannia in London. He imported in Paris the traditional Anglo-Saxon variety shows with tightrope walkers, conjurers, magicians, singers, and acrobats. The theater had undergone a complete refurbishment to modify stage and stalls. The new director was an Englishman called E. H. Neighbour. And it happened that Albert Capellani had spent several months in Great Britain, from January to August 1898.[4] This stay may have been part of his job for the bank; it certainly allowed him to learn some rudiments of English. While some American papers mention his knowledge of Shakespeare's tongue, it appears he could only just get by in English when he arrived in the United States in 1915.[5]

I do not know how Capellani joined the staff of the Alhambra. Nevertheless, he certainly had the necessary skills: he spoke some English and he was an accountant. He also loved folk songs. Among the few family papers are numerous songs written by his father, Charles. Also, the program of an amateur show on March 21, 1896, indicates Albert sang a light-hearted song entitled "Caprice de Pierrette" while his brother Paul, then aged eighteen, performed in a one-act play. Another anecdote suggests Albert's cheerful and jovial character. A Pathé cameraman, Pierre Trimbach, who was a friend and a colleague, mentioned that one day Capellani started singing *"Ah! Si tu voyais ton enfant, ma mère!"* (Ah, if you could see your child, mother!) when he saw him dressed in laboratory overalls.

A persistent myth is that Capellani worked for André Antoine or Firmin Gémier as an assistant or stage manager. No reliable sources confirm those assertions. It appears that the myth was born with Charles Ford's book.[6] Ford, however, offers no references, and his dating is totally unreliable. In his memoirs, Pierre Trimbach mentions Albert Capellani as being a "member of André Antoine's company."[7] But it's obvious that Trimbach confused Albert with Paul. In fact, in 1904, Paul Capellani made his debut at the Théâtre Antoine playing Edgar of Gloucester in Antoine's new production of *King Lear*. Several erroneous references in the French National Library catalog also mistakenly link Albert with Antoine. In the catalog, several plays staged by André Antoine mention Albert in the credits. When looking at the production stills, however, one realizes it's in fact Paul. The two brothers couldn't have looked more different. While Albert was stout, with a Mephistophelian beard and handlebar mustache, Paul was slim and wore a small mustache, which he shaved from time to time. In addition, Paul definitely worked with Firmin Gémier, in particular in Romain Rolland's *Quatorze Juillet,* which Gémier produced in 1902 at the Théâtre de la Renaissance.[8]

In his memoirs, André Antoine only mentions Paul Capellani as participating in various plays, such as *King Lear* (in a new translation by Pierre Loti) and Wilhelm Meyer-Förster's *Old Heidelberg* (with Sylvie as Käthie).[9] There is no trace of any correspondence between Albert and André Antoine. Paul Capellani, however, maintained a regular correspondence with Antoine and with his son André-Paul. He called Antoine "My dear boss" and his son "My dear friend." Furthermore, all the information on Albert Capellani found in census and electoral registers shows that from 1896 until 1902 he was an accountant, a bank clerk, or was otherwise employed by a bank (the Comptoir Municipal d'Escompte).

During this period, Paul's career development shows an artist who regularly contacted personalities from the stage. No sooner was he back from his military service than he sent a letter to writer Marcel Schwob—then married to actress Marguerite Moreno. Paul wrote, "I would be very happy to talk with you of my projects for next season and at the same time to listen to your advice, which is really important to me."[10] In 1922, he wrote with emotion to André Antoine, "The last days of rehearsal reminded me of the admirable period when we worked in Théâtre Antoine, which still remains the best of my life as an artist."[11]

Another person's testimony confirms that Albert Capellani had no stage experience of any kind. In 1948, when he was asked about his career at Pathé, actor Henri Etiévant said this about his director: "He was no actor, had no stage experience. He was a former secretary of the Alhambra."[12] Etiévant's testimony is crucial, as he worked closely with Antoine when he created the Théâtre Libre, then later in other theaters such as L'Odéon and L'Œuvre. If Albert Capellani had worked even for a short period for Antoine, Etiévant would have been aware of it.

In all the contemporary biographies of Albert I examined, Antoine is never mentioned, and neither is any stage experience. In the small biography published in 1912 in the weekly *Pathé-Journal,* only his experience as administrator of the Alhambra is mentioned. In the US trade movie directories from 1916 and 1917, there is no mention of any stage experience. The comparison with his brother's biography in the same directory is telling: it states that Paul attended the conservatory and worked at Théâtre Antoine. In the same directory, Maurice Tourneur mentioned his own work with Antoine. André Antoine was then world famous; surely Albert would have mentioned Antoine's name if he had ever worked with him.

During all those years, Paul's and Albert's biographies were confused. Paul's study at the conservatory was ascribed to Albert, as was Paul's working relationship with Antoine. Now we need not mix them up anymore. Moreover, a review of the archive of the daily newspaper *Le Petit Parisien* shows that the only Capellani ever mentioned was Paul, in the entertainment section. Albert was a shadowy figure and would remain so until 1915.

3

Pathé

When did Albert Capellani join Pathé? It is impossible to give a precise date, as the archives that could give us an answer do not exist anymore. If we trust the Pathé catalog produced by Henri Bousquet, Capellani's first film was *Le Chemineau*, a 110-meter dramatic scene, mentioned in the December 1905 *Pathé-Journal*. However, set designer Hughes Laurent mentioned in an article he wrote many years later that Capellani had directed a "scène à trucs" (scene with special effects) entitled *Le Prestidigitateur pratique*, which dated from July 1905.[1]

There is also the question of how the Alhambra administrator moved to Pathé and became a motion picture director. Capellani's biography in the *Pathé-Journal* stated that he "was administrator of the Alhambra when the Pathé Frères company asked him to join them as director."[2] It is easy to find a link between the Alhambra and Pathé. In their September 1905 program, we discover that the music hall showed "Animated pictures—New cinematographic pictures from the Pathé company." Movies were starting to leave the fairgrounds to join the variety shows. Capellani, as the administrator of the Alhambra, must have had useful contacts at Pathé.

According to Capellani's grandson Bernard Basset-Capellani, Ferdinand Zecca was the person who asked him to join Pathé. In any case, in those days, recruitments at Pathé were made by word of mouth. We find all sorts of atypical profiles among the employees. Ferdinand Zecca was first hired by Charles Pathé to record cylinders in 1896 because of his warm tones. Georges Monca, another contemporary director, was an actor at the Théâtre de la République, the future Alhambra. Georges Fagot was secretary to the president of the Seine department council before becoming secretary to Zecca. And one thing leading to another, Fagot later became title-writer, as film subtitles (intertitles) were called at the time.

There is one thing we can be sure of: Capellani was interested in motion pictures very early on. In 1923, he said in an interview, "I've been interested in cinema for twenty-two years."[3] His passion for animated pictures—starting in 1901—therefore predated his arrival at Pathé. According to Pierre Trimbach, his father, Charles, shared Albert's interest.[4]

When Capellani arrived at Pathé, the company with the proud rooster was the world leader in terms of motion picture production. Under Charles Pathé's direction, the company underwent a spectacular development. He created a vertically integrated company, which made its own film stock, produced pictures, and organized its films' distribution worldwide. In October 1906, between 33 and 50 percent of all films shown in American nickelodeons were French films from Pathé. That year, 1906, saw the opening of the Joinville-le-Pont factory and of the first major film studio, called the Vincennes theater. Film production was increasing, and Pathé was recruiting new directors. It was a pivotal period in film history. The narrative film was becoming the standard. Motion pictures would soon cease to be a fairground attraction and become entertainment in their own right. In this process, Charles Pathé was a precursor. He understood that to conquer new markets, he had to create outlets abroad. He also understood that he should control costs. Mass production was coming.

In 1907, Pathé revolutionized film distribution in creating the rental system. Previously, films were sold to exhibitors (often fairground people) and could be run until the film was completely worn out. Even so, selling films was often difficult. As Ferdinand Zecca noted, "Fairground people asked for multiple subjects, but they wanted them short, because of the price. One film would cost about two francs per meter. When a film worked well, we had to print twelve to fifteen hundred copies!"[5] The rental system changed film distribution completely. Movie theaters were starting to open—like the Omnia-Pathé in December 1906—and introduced a new audience to this form of entertainment. To extend its audience, motion pictures had to attract more affluent and literate spectators. In short, it needed to bring in the middle class as well as the working class. Distribution was to be controlled by a chain of permanent theaters. These principles of film distribution are the same today. As Ferdinand Zecca said in an interview in 1932, "It's only progressively that we were able to expand our subjects and our influence. Around 1907, I managed to make 305-meter pictures, but there was some resistance. When the first permanent theaters opened, when our exhibitors became sedentary, we abandoned the sale system for the rental and we were at last free to choose the length of our pictures."[6]

To attract new spectators for the movies, the quality had to fulfill audience expectations. At this stage, films were one-reelers and lasted about ten minutes. At Pathé, the company developed the narrative film, producing fairy tales, dramas, comedies, scenes with special effects, biblical stories, and historical dramatizations. Here we find all the future genres of today's motion pictures: melodrama, comedy, sword-and-sandal epic, historical costume drama, and so on.

We can get an idea of the atmosphere of film studios of the time thanks to interviews with many of the people who worked then for Pathé. The atmosphere sounded relaxed, and improvisation was their motto. Georges Fagot described humorously how they decided to make a comedy:

One winter morning, when arriving at the studio Rue du Bois, Albert Capellani tells us, "The lake in Saint-Mandé is frozen! It's our best opportunity to take a skating sequence."

"Yes, but something funny," approves Zecca. "Let's take somebody who can't skate." "Or who has never skated at all," concludes Capellani. "And somebody posh, so that it would look ridiculous," adds Zecca. And suddenly, hitting his forehead: "Of course! We need Max Linder!"

It was quite something. Max, wearing court shoes, striped pants, dinner jacket, and top hat, fell flat on his face. He didn't have to look confused; he had never put on skates in his life!

Les Débuts d'un patineur [1907, Louis Gasnier] was a tremendous success, and from then on the public never stopped loving Max Linder.[7]

This atmosphere of improvisation did not mean they spent freely. At Pathé, every expense was under control. When Max Linder asked for fifty francs to replace his shoes, it gave rise to a real debate. "They gave him the money," Fagot recalled, "but what discussions beforehand, what alarms and heartbreaks! At a time when you could get an excellent pair of shoes for fourteen francs fifty centimes, fifty francs seemed like a lot of money. But after all, it was his style that made Max such a comedian. We should have thought of that. It's a lack of commercial foresight to cut down on such small expenditures!"[8]

During 1906, Albert Capellani shot only nine movies. In those days, a movie was finished in just a few days. We can therefore assume that Capellani had other occupations besides being just a film director. A 1923 article mentions him as being the director of the Vincennes studios.[9] He must have had purely administrative tasks in Pathé. He would become the artistic director of the Société Cinématographique des Auteurs et Gens de Lettres (Cinematographic Society of Authors and Writers) later. But let's not get ahead of ourselves. For the moment, Capellani was a newcomer in the Pathé organization. He had to prove himself. Ferdinand Zecca was the man who controlled production, along with Charles Pathé. As director

Georges Monca recalled, "Every Monday morning, we had a conference. And we established the weekly schedule. Every Saturday afternoon, Mr. Pathé and Ferdinand Zecca examined the production and made their remarks."[10]

From 1905 to 1907, Capellani made about twenty films. At first, he concentrated on drama. One of his first films was an adaptation of the second book of Victor Hugo's *Les Misérables.* In *Le Chemineau,* he already demonstrates a real visual sense. A man walks under the snow in a wintry landscape. Rather than moving parallel to the camera, he walks directly towards it until his face appears in full close-up. The close-up was still uncommon in French films and still would be by the time Capellani left Pathé in 1914.

Capellani's comic sense was also put to use. He gave comedian André Deed his first part, in *Les Apprentissages de Boireau* (1907). Capellani noticed Deed's comic skills and launched his career in a whole series of films under the nickname "Boireau." In this first film, Boireau clumsily attempts to get a job as hatter, grocer, and hairdresser. Each time, he is kicked out after creating much havoc.

Capellani also directed some fairy tales *(scènes féeries et contes),* such as the delightful *La Légende de Polichinelle* (1907), where a clean-shaven Max Linder, in the title role, rides a small hobby horse in pursuit of a doll he has fallen in love with. The film alternates studio special effects—showing the brilliance of Segundo de Chomón, a master of the craft at Pathé—and location shooting around Pierrefonds castle.

The turning point in Capellani's career happened in 1908. He decided to adapt a French classic. Henri Desfontaines, who was then an actor for Pathé, recalled that "Albert Capellani had more ambition. And as he was fearless, he decided to adapt a masterpiece, Molière's *Don Juan,* quite simply! Paul Capellani was to play Don Juan and me, Sganarelle. It happened as Capellani had planned it. I cannot remember what the film looked like, but it must have been a success because it opened the eyes of two businessmen of the first order, [Pierre] Decourcelle and [Eugène] Gugenheim, who created a company whose aim was to adapt to the screen the most famous works of literature and of the stage, La Société Cinématographique des Auteurs et Gens de Lettres."[11]

4

The Société Cinématographique des Auteurs et Gens de Lettres

The creation of the Société Cinématographique des Auteurs et Gens de Lettres (SCAGL) was actually a far more complex process than Henri Desfontaines described. There was indeed a desire to create a company to adapt great literary works. But this desire was not just in the minds of Pierre Decourcelle and Eugène Gugenheim. The will behind it was also that of Charles Pathé. Decourcelle and Gugenheim were two famous playwrights who knew the Parisian stage inside out. Their contacts would prove useful as they recruited authors both living and dead, the latter via the deceased writers' official heirs. Decourcelle had been corresponding for years with various leaders of the theater, such as André Antoine. He also knew numerous actors, including Mévisto, whose real name was Auguste-Marie Wistaux. A disciple of Antoine since the creation of the Théâtre Libre, Mévisto would also work at SCAGL. Decourcelle's address book would prove invaluable in recruiting the cream of Parisian theaters and music halls.

The creation of this Pathé subsidiary was in embryonic form as early as the spring of 1908. On March 10 of that year, the sons of Bernard Merzbach, bankers who were among the main Pathé shareholders, wrote to Victor Hugo's executor,

Gustave Simon, requesting exclusive rights to various Hugo works. They sought to develop a new market in adapting great literary works, a market they believed would be profitable. To avoid future conflicts, they assured Gustave Simon that "full satisfaction will be given to him to safeguard the literary interest which he is invested with, thanks to the presence of writers in any company formed to make movies as in our contract."[1] Pierre Decourcelle wrote Simon on the same date to assure that his financial demands would be examined and a special safeguard clause would be added to the contract stipulating and guaranteeing Hugo's executor "that two subjects at least taken from Victor Hugo works will be presented annually."[2] On June 11, 1908, Simon received, by recorded delivery, the SCAGL contract. The new company had no letterhead yet and used that of Bernard Merzbach's sons. On June 17, Merzbach's sons announced the creation of SCAGL, a public company with a capital of 500,000 francs and Charles Pathé as its president.[3] Two days later, Decourcelle sent a letter to Simon asking him to come to discuss a proposed adaptation, giving him an appointment at the company headquarters at 68 Rue de la Chaussée d'Antin. The letter had a simple stamp serving as heading.[4] This correspondence shows that SCAGL was created with prior work to acquire film rights from famous authors.

If Charles Pathé had wanted to create this subsidiary company, it was also for economic reasons. The accounts of the two companies were going to be kept separate. Thus, SCAGL would be able to make savings on taxes, as shown in a letter sent by SCAGL's secretary to the Prefect in 1914 to obtain tax relief: "We are not a distributor of films or stills; the unique object of our company is to *photograph* films for the Compagnie Générale des Etablissements Pathé-Frères, which *develops the negatives* that we exposed. I would therefore be grateful if you report the former registered company occupation and, in consequence, give us the tax relief owed us for the year 1914." The secretary quotes the contract with Pathé: "Positive films coming from the SCAGL negative films, established as above, will be sold to the Compagnie Générale des Etablissements Pathé-Frères, which has the absolute exclusive distribution rights of all negatives produced by SCAGL."[5]

At the same time, the Film d'Art company was also being created. Its main interest was also the adaptation of literary works, and it was also looking for authors. November 17, 1908, the day of the premiere of its film *L'Assassinat du Duc de Guise,* is often cited as the birthdate of the artistic motion picture. However, SCAGL beat it at the finish line in presenting its production of *L'Arlésienne* on October 1 of that year at the Omnia-Pathé theater. This version of Alphonse Daudet's *L'Arlésienne* was directed by Albert Capellani, and it was a genuine masterpiece. The film was considered lost for many decades until its recent resurrection at the Bologna Film Festival in 2011. *L'Arlésienne* was longer than usual for the time: it was a 355-meter picture, with a running time of about 18 minutes.

L'Arlésienne was shot almost entirely on location in Arles. In it we discover the old streets, the Roman amphitheater then used as a bullring, and the vast olive groves. Capellani shows a remarkable sense of pictorialism in his camera angles and lighting effects. The film even contains an astonishing 180-degree panorama. He uses double exposures with amazing virtuosity. Capellani manages to make us feel Frédéric's torments as he is haunted by the image of the Arlésienne, which appears constantly by his side, even in the presence of his bride. The film captures the poetry of Daudet's work. This first adaptation of a classic was a masterstroke. However, the future director Henri Desfontaines, who played the part of Mitifio, had mixed memories from the shooting: a complete novice, he had to ride a horse, and suffered a nasty fall, which he remembered for years.[6]

Albert Capellani had been sent by Pathé to SCAGL to become its artistic director. He spent most of his time in the new SCAGL studios, situated in the appropriately named 1 Rue de la Cinématographie in Vincennes. As artistic director Capellani had multiple duties. According to surviving documents and contemporary testimonies, he not only directed pictures, he also handled complaints from authors' legal heirs, supervised the tests to select new cameramen, prepared screen adaptations (sometimes with Pierre Decourcelle), and provided cue sheets for editing. He left Paris and moved back to Vincennes, at 2 Rue Lebeau. His second child, his daughter Simonne, was born there on February 5, 1908.

After this marvelous *Arlésienne* Capellani shot another remarkable picture, *L'Homme aux gants blancs* (1908). This movie contains one of the first examples of triptych split screen. A high-society robber asks a hotel employee to order him white gloves. The employee then calls a glover. At this point, the screen is divided into three parts, with the two people on the phone at left and right and, in the center, a view of the Avenue de l'Opéra. This film, a detective story, is particularly well structured. The society robber is exposed because of his white gloves and accused of a murder he did not commit. The film ends on an ironical note, as the real murderer watches the robber being taken away by the police. The tone and cinematographic qualities of *L'Homme aux gants blancs* shows a filmmaker already confident in his art and ahead of his time. In comparison, D. W. Griffith was just starting to shoot his first picture, *The Adventures of Dollie* (1908), which has none of the sophistication shown by Capellani.

The best witness from this period was Pierre Trimbach. He had joined SCAGL thanks to Capellani, first as a lab technician in charge of film processing in 1908. Then, in 1909, he was offered the job of assistant cameraman to De Marsan. After a period of training, he had to undergo an examination in front of Charles Pathé, Ferdinand Zecca, cameraman René Guichard, and Capellani. He had to shoot a scene with Jean Angelo and Stacia Napierkowska and later answer a technical questionnaire. To celebrate his successful completion of the exam, the whole troupe went to lunch in the restaurant Le Cygne (The Swan), on the Avenue de Paris in Vincennes.

Shooting of the movies took place principally in the morning, from nine o'clock to noon. Most of the performers were also stage actors who had to attend theater rehearsals in the afternoon. Afternoons at SCAGL were spent preparing the sets. For major pictures, however, the shooting would be continuous. The actors were not under contract as they were at Gaumont; instead, they were paid a fee per day of work. Only technicians and directors were under contract. This provided undeniable savings in the long term.

The SCAGL "shooting theater," as the studio was called at the time, offered all the latest modern conveniences in terms of lighting. They had the famous Cooper-Hewitt mercury tubes and Sunlight arcs. The building was constructed with a glass wall on one side. The roof was also made of glass. To have the light coming only from one side allowed easier setups for the cameramen than if the building were made entirely of glass. The set was equipped with numerous trap doors to shoot special-effects sequences. There was even a pool, fifteen meters by ten, to shoot water sequences.

In this intensely creative environment, SCAGL production underwent an exponential growth, in terms of quantity as well as quality. During the period February 1910 until March 1911, Albert Capellani directed no fewer than twenty-five pictures. On the surviving register from that period, we see he was constantly shooting pictures with only one or two days' break between them.[7] Movies were still short. For example, the shooting of *L'Intrigante* (working title: *L'Institutrice*), a 275-meter drama (about ten minutes), took just four days, from December 6 to December 9, 1910. The main actress, Catherine Fonteney, was paid 30 francs per day. The result was a very clever movie, which has fortunately survived. It was about a little orphan girl who is tormented by her Machiavellian tutor, played by Catherine Fonteney, who seems to have been type-cast in this kind of role.[8] The little girl manages to expose the schemer by photographing her through a peephole. Her father then realizes he had been manipulated by the evil creature. The total cost of this movie was 295 francs, about one franc per meter of film.

The studio was empty during summertime. The heat under the artificial lights was unbearable. Taking advantage of the situation, Capellani went on holiday. Nevertheless, even on holiday, he received letters from the SCAGL secretary asking for a cue sheet to edit a film. He decided not to reply. After all, he was on holiday. The secretary understood his attitude. Administrative tasks must have been heavy, however, because as of January 1911, each director was given an assistant, who would reply to the mail and manage invoices from suppliers. All the props used on the set—wigs, furniture, dishes, and so on—were rented. But, as usual, to save money, the studio did not recruit a professional for the job of director's assistant. They just used a character actor, who received a meager salary of 5 or 10 francs a day. Thus, Paul Adolphe Tabutiaux, nick-named A. Polthy, became Capellani's assistant while still working as an extra.[9]

In 1910, the studio was working at full capacity with a stable of directors including Capellani, Georges Denola, Michel Carré, and Georges Monca (who directed mainly the Rigadin comedy series with comedian Charles Prince).[10] Six cameramen were under contract, besides Pierre Trimbach: Le Forestier, René Guichard, Karénine Mérobian, Alfred Guichard, Marsan, and Mario. The company regularly used the services of famous stage actors, such as Gabrielle Robinne (paid 50 francs per day), Henry-Krauss (50 francs), Henri Etiévant (30 francs), Mistinguett (60 francs), Stacia Napierkowska (50 francs), and Paul Capellani (40 francs).[11] The fee varied according to the fame of the actor.

Paul Capellani had by this time become a star of the Paris

stage and worked with Firmin Gémier, André Antoine, and Lucien Guitry. If proof was ever needed of his fame, his photograph appeared in the albums of Robert de Montesquiou, who was then Marcel Proust's friend and the model for the Baron de Charlus.[12] This enlightened aesthete, who loved the theater, made scrapbooks of actors' and actresses' photographs as well as drawings of famous set decorators. Paul started working for the motion pictures at Pathé in 1908. He later recalled that his first film was *L'Enlisé du Mont-Saint-Michel* (1908); he also noted that he created a sculpture inspired by the film.[13] He went on working for SCAGL until 1914, under the direction of his brother and others.

In several European countries, films were becoming longer. In Denmark, Urban Gad had directed the superb *Afgrunden* (*The Abyss*, 1910) with Asta Nielsen, which ran 40 minutes. However, Capellani was ahead of the Dane with *L'Assommoir*, a 740-meter film (about 40 minutes), which was screened for a gala premiere in December 1908 at the Cirque d'Hiver in Paris together with *L'Assassinat du Duc de Guise* (1908). (It went on general release only in April 1909.) This film is considered the first feature in French cinema. This adaptation of Zola was released in the United States in October 1909 and was appropriately entitled *Drink*. The movie was essentially propaganda against alcoholism. And this was how the Americans received it: a reviewer wrote that the film "is an intensely powerful argument in favor of, not merely temperance, but of prohibition."[14]

Capellani's *L'Assommoir* has aged extremely well. It combines cleverly staged studio sequences with location shots, set in the streets of Paris and a *guinguette*.[15] The film's title credits name the theater where each actor worked. This was one of the trademarks of SCAGL for advertising its productions. By contrast, not a single technician's name was mentioned, not even the director's. The film offers excellent social realism, which certainly owed a lot to Capellani. American audiences were particularly impressed with the final scene, which, one reviewer noted, "is one of intense power, and the actor who took the part of the maddened Coupeau was a very strong performer, for he seemed to get into the very skin of the part and to suggest, according to conceptions of it, the very reality of delirium tremens. But, indeed, the whole play is convincingly acted right through. The quarrel between the two women is the subplot of the piece. It starts in a laundry, advances a stage when the wicked woman loosens the scaffold from which Coupeau falls, and reaches its culminating point in the death chamber of the maddened drunkard. It goes without saying that all the parts in the piece are superbly acted and that the photography of it is up to Pathé standard."[16]

The script condensed the storyline of Zola's novel. Virginie (Catherine Fonteney) is the pivotal character in the film. To avenge herself for the beating given by Gervaise (Eugénie Nau), she does not hesitate to make Coupeau (Alexandre Arquillières) have an accident, and even to kill him by substituting absinthe (the poison of the times) for wine. Coupeau's death scene seems a trifle overacted to modern eyes, but it did not bother the American critics unduly.

In 1911, the first adaptation of Hugo's *The Hunchback of Notre-Dame* (*Notre-Dame de Paris*), running 810 meters (about 40 minutes) was made. The studio always assigned Albert Capellani to its longest and most prestigious pictures, and accordingly, he was given this Victor Hugo adaptation. For this particular feature, the company did not skimp on sets or extras. The total cost was higher than for ordinary pictures: 6,836 francs (8 francs per meter). The film was shot entirely in the studio. For the famous scene when Esmeralda (Stacia Napierkowska) brings water to Quasimodo (Henry-Krauss), who has been sentenced to the stocks, a set measuring 10 meters by 18 was built. A painted backdrop was used for the sky; Notre-Dame cathedral was cut out in thick cardboard, and the surrounding houses gave depth to the whole set. No fewer than sixty-five extras were used, and the sequence was shot with two cameras: one on a parallel for high-angle shots, and the second for long shots. The latter was operated by Pierre Trimbach.[17]

Unfortunately, the film is disappointing. Most of the sets lack depth, and scenes are marred by the obviously painted backdrops (except for the sequence mentioned above). Henry-Krauss wears rather comical makeup, and the narrative is focused on Esmeralda at the expense of Quasimodo, a fault also of the 1923 *Hunchback of Notre-Dame*, directed by Wallace Worsley. Stacia Napierkowska, originally a dancer, sways and constantly aims to attract the libidinous Claude Frollo (Claude Garry), who waves his arms like a bat. One sequence is memorable, a sadistic torture sequence, where Esmeralda writhes in pain while Frollo seems to enjoy it. Location shooting would have given the picture a far more realistic look.

Capellani often shot on location in the streets of Paris, without even asking for official authorization from the head of the Parisian police. Journalist Adrien Vély described the shooting of a 300-meter comedy entitled *Pour voir Paris* (1911), which was made in such a way. The film tells the story of an innocent young girl from Pont-Aven in Brittany, freshly arrived in Paris, who discovers the modern Babylon. She gets robbed of her money by an *apache* (as hooligans were called at the time) before being hassled by an aging Romeo. Eventually she is saved by a policeman from back home, who takes her to the train station. The filmmakers decided to shoot at Gare de l'Est (the train station for eastern destinations in Paris) rather than Montparnasse station (where trains from Brittany arrive), as they felt they would get better light at Gare de l'Est and because the employees there were more benevolent toward film crews. The camera was set up right in front of the exit for suburban train arrivals so that the actress playing the lead (Suzanne Goldstein) could mix with the crowd of travelers. Unfortunately, she ended up being surrounded by young vagrants trying to woo her. Then the shot was spoiled by passersby, who gathered around the lens. The crew was forced to retreat, hiding inside a subway station for a few minutes before restarting the filming. A policeman left them to it. "I was sure you didn't have [official authorization]," he told the filmmakers. "Nobody ever does. . . . That's why I waited until you'd finished to ask you for one."[18]

The move toward feature-length films was now unstoppable. SCAGL was planning to launch a titanic project: a motion picture over 3,400 meters long. Albert Capellani was going to direct *Les Misérables*.

5

Les Misérables

SCAGL was taking a big risk in producing a film with the unusual length of 3,445 meters—that is, a picture lasting more than three hours.[1] The risk would prove worthwhile, both in France and abroad. The film would be shown in four "episodes," at weekly intervals.

We do not know who made the decision to produce such a feature. But it seems obvious that Charles Pathé must have been the one who gave the go-ahead for such a risky and costly project. Pierre Decourcelle used his considerable connections to recruit famous actors and worked with Capellani on the adaptation of the novel. The latter directed the film and had to deal with the fuss created by Victor Hugo's executor. Yet Capellani's name would not be mentioned—as was the case ever since he started in SCAGL—not in the film's credits nor in its advertising. In those days, the director of a film was not considered important. Publicity mainly centered around the producing company (Pathé, Gaumont, SCAGL, Film d'Art, etc.) and on the actors. Nevertheless, in the weekly *Pathé-Journal*, which was designed for theater exhibitors, some directors, including Camille de Morlhon, Henri Andréani, and Alfred Machin, were starting to be mentioned. The name of Albert Capellani, however, who was in fact a prime mover inside the company, never appeared, except for a brief biographical article in a 1912 issue. For the first time, the journal acknowledged that SCAGL "owes its prestige to Cappelani, who remains, in spite of his modesty, the jewel in its crown."[2]

The article also provided a list of films directed by Capellani, though that list, unfortunately, was unreliable. Indeed, it mentioned *Athalie* (1910) as being one of Capellani's films. Yet in the surviving SCAGL register, Michel Carré is named as director.[3] We should therefore note that neither Pathé nor SCAGL would be inclined to promote a director, unless he asked specifically for it. Capellani did not look for any such credit. In the interviews he gave in the following years, we perceive a craftsman proud of his work, but not looking for fame. He remained a simple, easily accessible figure, and the modesty mentioned in the *Pathé-Journal* article seemed to be real.

For *Les Misérables,* SCAGL was not going to be stingy. The total cost of the film would reach 50,000 francs for the actors' fees alone. The company had paid 180,000 francs to acquire the adaptation rights of the book from Victor Hugo's legal heirs.[4] Despite winning this enormous sum, Victor Hugo's executor, Gustave Simon, would create problems during the shooting.

Most sequences were shot on outdoor locations. For the barricade scenes, the filmmakers re-created the houses of an Old Paris street—the Rue des Lions in the Marais district—building them life size next to the Vincennes studios. In order to get all the details right, Pierre Trimbach and his colleagues went on location to take stills of old houses, doors, and stones. From those photographs, the set designers rebuilt an entire street of Paris in Vincennes. Trimbach mentioned a huge set measuring 40 by 22 meters. Once it was completed, everybody examined the sky worriedly: the magnificent set could be destroyed with a single shower.

When shooting the barricade sequence, technicians arrived at 6:00 a.m. to prepare everything. Around 7:30 a.m., ninety extras arrived to play the soldiers and the rioters. Then, finally, between 8:00 and 9:00 a.m., the lead actors arrived. These included Henry-Krauss (Jean Valjean), Mistinguett (Eponine), Gabriel de Gravone (Marius), Henri Etiévant (Javert), and little Gaudin (Gavroche). After two rehearsals, the barricade sequence was shot, using two cameras. Celebrities from both the artistic and the political world came to visit the set of the prestigious film—painter André Derain, politician André Tardieu, and minister Paul Painlevé, among others. André Antoine, a friend of Pierre Decourcelle, also occasionally visited. Many actors employed by SCAGL were members of Antoine's theater company.

For the midday break, Capellani ordered a cold lunch for the artists. Around 1:00 p.m., the owner of The Swan restaurant—a favorite with Pathé employees—brought some large baskets full of provisions. Everybody filled a disposable plate and ate their lunch in a few minutes before going back to work until 6:00 p.m. When the day's shooting was over, the rushes went immediately to the processing lab. As soon as the director and the technicians had their mind put at rest by screening the rushes, everybody departed to The Swan for a well-deserved dinner.

On June 25, 1912, with the first part of the film already filmed, Victor Hugo's executor inserted himself into the proceedings with a letter to Capellani:

My Dear Friend,

I learned that *Les Misérables* has already been cast, and even rehearsed in parts. The film company, defying convention, is failing to honor its commitments, as our contracts stipulate. I have the "right to control sets, cast and staging," which is logical, as I am responsible to the public for the screen adaptation of Victor Hugo's works. Thus, I reserve the right to prohibit the film's release on the grounds of violation of these commitments.

Yours truly,
Gustave Simon[5]

Capellani replied very calmly to quench this fire:

Dear Mr. Simon,

Tomorrow—on Tuesday—I'm starting the second reel of the second part of *Les Misérables* (the Picpus convent sequence). I worked on it with Mr. Decourcelle on Saturday, for the better part of the day, and it's working. It wasn't easy, as the story with the two coffins is rather confusing, cinematographically speaking. Unfortunately, I do not have any time to come and see you. I hope you will accept my apologies. I know you are also very busy, so I do not dare ask you to come to Rue Louis Le Grand tonight between 6:00 and 7:00 p.m. Nevertheless, if you come tomorrow I can read you the script in ten minutes. You can rely entirely on me, as I am sure you know, and I promise you a beautiful thing.

Yours sincerely,
A. Capellani

If you can phone me upon receiving this letter and tell me where you are tonight at 5:30 p.m., I will try to go to your place.[6]

At 4:00 that day, not having received any phone call, Capellani asked his assistant, A. Polthy, to send a telegram to Simon, saying that he was shooting all day the following day. This was the last straw for an already irritated Gustave Simon. He sent Capellani a menacing letter the very next day.

My Dear Capellani,

I wrote you I would come to Vincennes at 9:30 a.m. . . . My intention was to come to Vincennes not to work, but to tell you this: Mr. Pierre Decourcelle told me expressly that the first part [of the film] was very good, that I would be able to screen the reels and if I didn't like them, they would be modified according

to my desires in terms of scenes or in terms of actors.
. . . I am opposed to the shooting of the second reel
of the second part of *Les Misérables* (the Picpus
convent sequence) until the preceding reels are
shown to me. If you pay no heed, I retain the option
to claim my rights in a tribunal. A dispatch from Mr.
Polthy telling me the shooting was going on for the
whole day in Vincennes made me decide not to go
to Vincennes, as this development indicated you
were not taking into account the reasons I
mentioned. . . . [7]

The rest of the correspondence has not survived. But in
December of the same year, Simon wrote to a woman, who
must certainly be Victor Hugo's granddaughter, about screen
adaptations of Hugo's works. In that letter, he conceded defeat,
telling her, "When six or seven months ago, you evinced some
alarm about motion pictures in connection with the tour of *Les
Misérables,* which was already going on, I told you not to worry
as the picture was not made yet. . . . Since then, the film has
been finished as well as *Notre-Dame de Paris.*"[8]

Simon was mainly worried that the motion picture release
would coincide with a touring stage adaptation of the novel.
This worry was probably groundless: the film release would
generate such publicity as to boost sales of the novel, and, no
doubt, also tickets for the stage adaptation.

We know very little about the way Capellani directed his
actors in those days. Henri Etiévant, who played Javert, remembered: "He was a very intelligent man whose capacity to assimi-
late his work was remarkable. He had the full confidence of
Decourcelle and Gugenheim. . . . We had a vague screenplay of
a few lines, describing what was happening. And we staged it
ourselves. And Capellani was there to say, 'That's all right' or
'that's no good. It's too long, it's too short.' But he gave us a
lot of freedom in terms of initiative. . . . *Les Misérables* was

made like that, between us, with the novel in hand."[9] Etiévant's testimony depicts a director who gave his actors freedom to improvise, but who nevertheless controlled the pacing of a sequence. Another skill not mentioned by Etiévant was Capellani's visual sense in terms of composition. His *Les Misérables* shows a faultless dramatic and narrative sense for such a long feature, while other filmmakers of the time were still groping in the dark.

Advertising for the picture centered on Victor Hugo. His huge portrait was surrounded by a slogan claiming, "Nobody wants to miss the dramatic epic in four episodes and nine parts, played by the elite of Paris artists: Miss Ventura, Mistinguett, Eugénie Nau, etc. Mr. Henry-Krauss, Etiévant, Milo, etc. Every schoolteacher, every parent and head of household will want to see and show children this lesson in heroism and goodness."[10]

The film was released in four parts in December 1912, giving a more reasonable screening time to an audience not accustomed to such lengthy features. The film's success in France was enormous, and it would also be celebrated in the United States, where it was distributed by Eclectic Film Company, a Pathé subsidiary. Large, double-page advertisements decorated trade magazines for American exhibitors, announcing the arrival "of the classic feature that will take the world by storm."[11] The reviews were excellent; a typical notice stated: "There are many fine things in this photoplay: some artistic double exposures, picturesque interiors of striking fidelity, admirably chosen interiors of decided educational merit. . . . The fine conception and unwavering grasp of details of Hugo's masterpiece displayed in every member of the cast is delightful throughout the whole twelve reels. One's interest never fails for a moment. In fact, this is one of the things that stamp this great picture play a masterpiece throughout. The Valjean of Mr. Krauss dominates by its majestic strength."[12] The film was well received by the public and played for months at the

Carnegie Lyceum in New York before being distributed across the country.[13]

As in France, Albert Capellani's name was not mentioned anywhere as director of *Les Misérables*. Yet it was thanks to this film that Capellani would get a foothold in the American film industry in 1915.

6

Filmmaker

The "visualizer of *Les Misérables*," as the Americans would call Capellani, was now the main director at SCAGL. His financial status was now secure, and he and his family moved in 1912 to Saint-Mandé, an affluent city near Vincennes. The family grew again with the birth of a third child, Odette, on June 2, 1912.

It is interesting to note how Capellani defined his job through the years. In 1905, when he was still the Alhambra administrator, his son Roger's birth certificate stated that Capellani was a simple "employee." In 1908, with Simonne's birth, he wrote "playwright." Finally, in the 1911 Vincennes census, he wrote "*cinématographiste*," the term used at the time for filmmaker (or for any technician working in the motion picture industry). Movies were now important enough not to be considered a poor substitute for the legitimate stage. And Capellani declared proudly that he was a filmmaker. In fact, he was the first person in France to direct a feature film longer than 3,000 meters (that is, with a running time of over two and a half hours). Pathé's main rival, Gaumont, would not produce such a feature until 1913, the year after *Les Misérables*, with Léonce Perret's *L'Enfant de Paris* (2,325 meters). Unlike Pathé, Gaumont preferred original stories written directly for the screen, in order to avoid having to pay adaptation rights— even if some of the scripts blatantly plagiarized famous novels and plays. Perret was another important and innovative film- maker of the time. With his cameraman Georges Specht, he developed backlighting effects and the practice of shooting on location. His *Enfant de Paris* made brilliant use of the Paris streets and of the Nice landscape in this story of kidnapping, which was full of twists and turns. Perret brought a poetic touch to his work, which differentiated him from his colleague, Louis Feuillade.

As a filmmaker, Capellani depicted events that showed him to be a man in touch with his time. At the beginning of 1912, a criminal gang was making headlines in the French press. The Bonnot gang introduced to France the American-style holdup. Using cars, they committed numerous burglaries and bank robberies. In a space of a few months, eight innocent people died from gunshot wounds. Their criminal saga ended on April 28, 1912, in Choisy-le-Roi (a suburb near Vincennes), with a siege involving hundreds of people.

Capellani had been tipped off to the showdown by an inspector from police headquarters whom he knew well. He asked his cameramen Marsan and Pierre Trimbach to come to his office on Saturday night, as they worked to prepare for the Monday morning shooting of a film. Instead, Capellani asked them to get ready to go to film the siege the very next morning. Capellani took the two cameramen in his car at 4:30 a.m. and drove them to Choisy-le-Roi. There they met a police officer who told them where the assault would take place. They stopped at a distance of 160 yards from a housing development, where Bonnot and his gang were hiding in a garage. Marsan and Trimbach hid behind trees with their cameras, ready to crank. They were surrounded by plainclothes policemen and by gendarmes equipped with rifles. As dawn broke, they managed to shoot a few meters of film before the start of the assault. Two or three policemen entered the house, and gunshots were heard. The gang shot back, and one of them was killed. The gunfire intensified. At that point, the cameramen filmed the arrival of the head of Parisian police, Louis Lépine, who would decide the next move. An army officer suggested blowing up the garage with explosives. In due course, the wall exploded, and the policemen ran inside. Bonnot, the gang leader, was wounded and eventually died. Marsan and

Trimbach managed to film everything, except for the scenes inside the house. To their everlasting regret, however, their work was never shown in the Pathé newsreels. A year later, on meeting a police inspector hired as adviser for a film, Trimbach learned that Lépine had screened the film and refused to allow its release. Presumably he did not want the general public to witness such a violent police action.

This newsreel was not the only innovative adventure involving Capellani. At one point he wanted to shoot dance or opera sequences with some double exposure over a black velvet background. These sequences would be accompanied by an orchestra, the one used by Pathé Frères to record music in their gramophone factory in Chatou. In 1913, Capellani decided to film a Hindu dance, featuring a young and beautiful soloist with long brown hair. It is likely that Claude Debussy was hired to write the score; the composer showed great interest in the new art form and knew Pierre Decourcelle well. Dressed in an Indian sari, the beautiful creature with her golden eyes and her long hair fascinated the young cameraman, Pierre Trimbach. They shot the sequence with various lighting effects to make her appear naked in silhouette behind a gray canvas. This thirty-seven-year-old Dutch dancer was named Margaretha Zelle. On October 15, 1917, she would be shot by a firing squad in the nearby moat of Vincennes fortress. Her stage name was Mata Hari. Unfortunately, this particular film remains lost.

At the end of 1911, Emile Pathé, who was in charge of Pathé's gramophone manufacturing, came to see Capellani and Decourcelle. He told them that he would like to make a short film with synchronized sound showing a singer singing a song; the music and the singing would be recorded beforehand on disc. Pathé did not want to leave the whole market of talking pictures to Gaumont, whose "Phonoscènes" had by then been in production for a number of years.

All those innovations, however, were only diversions from the studio's main product. Capellani continued to make feature films, such as his adaptation of a best seller, Jean Richepin's *La Glu* (1913).[1] (SCAGL produced adaptations of best sellers as well as literary classics.) For the title role, they hired the music-hall star Mistinguett, who played with great skill the mischievous man-eater nicknamed "The Glue." The tone of the film was unusual for the times. While the storyline was pure melodrama, it was played tongue-in-cheek throughout.

Richepin's novel was not meant to be taken completely seriously. The story of his plain-faced courtesan, Fernande, sounded like a lighthearted spoof of novels depicting rural France—in this case, fishermen in Brittany. Fernande (Mistinguett) marries Doctor Cézambre (Henry-Krauss) for money before leaving him to seduce other men for money, like the great French courtesans of the time. Having accumulated a small fortune, Fernande takes a holiday in Brittany and so beguiles a young fisherman named Marie-Pierre (Paul Capellani) that he forgets his bride (Cécile Guyon). "The Glue" ends up being killed by Marie-Pierre's mother in order to release her son from this woman's claws.

Several sequences in the film played melodramatic clichés to the hilt. Nevertheless, the performances avoided over-the-top posturing and remained perfectly natural. Mistinguett was perfect casting for Fernande. While she could not be considered beautiful according to the standard canon of beauty, she had a certain charm and a personality that transcended the screen and never failed to captivate an audience. Her tango in the Pré-Catelan restaurant showed her great virtuosity. Paul Capellani displayed real range as the innocent fisherman. He never overplays the naïve Marie-Pierre, even though he is completely spellbound by the siren, and manages to convey the young man's simplicity and artlessness through a minimum of expressions. Much of the film was shot in the small fishing harbor of Le Croisic in Brittany, giving a convincing background to the proceedings. The filmmakers also used a villa by the sea (still visible today in Le Croisic) for Fernande's holiday retreat, and filmed the picturesque walled city of Guérande, close to the coast.

The shooting of the final sequence in the studio was not without danger. The actress playing the mother wielded an inadequately padded hammer to strike Fernande, and poor Mistinguett collapsed on the floor. Fortunately, she was not seriously injured.[2]

If modern audiences do not fail to notice the humor and laugh good-naturedly, a contemporary American review showed it was not lost on the film's original audiences, either. Released in the United States in August 1914 under the title *The Siren*, the melodrama got a warm appreciation. The review in *Moving Picture World* stated, "The story is not all gray in its color. There are lighter touches, as, for instance, when Fernande, in Paris, is surrounded by her wildly competing admirers. Her affections are of the moment and are transferred from one to another without apparent rhyme or reason. Her dancing provides unexpected entertainment. Also her simulated drowning, when, clad in her one-piece bathing suit, in waist-deep water she calls for Pierre to save her, may provoke a smile."[3]

La Glu's cut negative was delivered to Pathé laboratories on October 1, 1913, and the film was released in cinemas in early November. Thus was the efficiency and speed of editing, processing, and printing in those days. Unlike *Les Misérables*, the film was not aimed at the general public. The newspaper *Le Petit Parisien* noted that, "owing to the rather special nature of this work—whose philosophical value will nevertheless not escape anybody—*La Glu* will be replaced for the Sunday and Thursday matinees by pictures more appropriate to the family audiences of these matinees."[4]

One month before *La Glu*, an adaptation of Zola's *Germinal*, running 3,020 meters, was released. This film is arguably Capellani's greatest work. Unlike *Les Misérables*, *Germinal* was a feature designed to be shown in a single screening. Capellani had therefore to maintain dramatic tension from start to finish. The picture managed to combine brilliantly naturalism, documentary-like sequences, and a real visual sense. This is precisely the type of movie that can still capture the interest of a modern spectator, even one who is not a fan of silent movies.

The total cost of the film was relatively high: 33,000 francs (more than 10 francs per meter). But the shooting schedule was rather short. We cannot give the actual dates, as this information has not been preserved. Nevertheless, we know that Henry-Krauss, who played the lead character of Etienne Lantier, received thirty-five fees, including eight for the location shooting in Auchel. Considering he appeared in virtually all the scenes, we can therefore gather the picture must have been shot in about thirty-five to forty-five days, a remarkably short time for a movie of such length.

The cameraman, Pierre Trimbach, tells us that Capellani took the set designers and operators to Auchel in the North of France, where he had a friend who was a mining engineer. They visited the mines with a foreman (called *porion*) and went down the pit in the colliery wagons used by the miners. It was impossible to take stills underground; the use of magnesium flare was prohibited. Pasquier, one of the assistant designers, took drawings of all the galleries. Outside, Trimbach took still pictures of the pithead, in order to be able to re-create it later in the studio. As usual, the sets were built with strong cardboard and wood board. The set, about fifty meters deep, was built in the same field where the barricades of *Les Misérables* had been. Up to 130 extras would be used for one particular sequence. The rehearsals for such a scene sometimes took the whole morning. Capellani decided to forgo lunch: they had to shoot the sequence quickly in case a shower destroyed their beautiful set. He did well to work fast. By 4:00 p.m., it was raining cats and dogs, and the pithead was destroyed.

Even if Trimbach did not mention it, some of the actors

went to Auchel to film some sequences. Henry-Krauss spent eight days there, and Sylvie (who played Catherine Maheu) four days. One of the major sequences shot on location was the fairground scene. Capellani very cleverly mixed his actors with onlookers. Some people at the fairgrounds actually stopped and stared at this intriguing camera that was observing them. The actors mixed with the crowd and went unnoticed. The resulting film has a quasi-documentary naturalism, giving it a powerful emotional impact. A modern spectator has the feeling of seeing Zola's characters in their daily environment. Similarly, Lantier's arrival at the mine is a great moment: we discover the slagheap, the miners' terraced house, the colliery wagons, and the pit with a superb panoramic view. For once, the studio sets matched the actual locations in terms of depth and realism, and any discrepancy is minimal.

The main characters' acting skill contributes to the film's realism. Henry-Krauss portrays Lantier with a subtlety of expression that seems almost unthinkable for a picture of that time. Indeed, the actors had to express their feelings essentially in long shot; there were no close-ups to highlight facial expressions. Opposite Henry-Krauss, Sylvie was an extraordinary Catherine Maheu. There is a genuine chemistry between the two characters each time they meet. Dressed as a man, she manages to fool Lantier. When she removes her headscarf to reveal her long mane of hair, Lantier's astonishment makes it one of the best sequences of the movie.

Capellani took all scenes in master shot; yet he gave deep focus to each sequence. He juxtaposed several simultaneous actions. During the miners' union meeting, when Lantier is making a speech on a platform at the back of the room, we can observe in the foreground what the anarchist, Souvarine, is up to. Each extra was given a precise action to perform in order to reinforce the realism of the scene. Catherine's death at the bottom of the pit retains its emotional power. Capellani did not look for sentimentality or sordid realism. He showed us human beings with their failures, human beings who loved and suffered. The film ends on a hopeful note as Lantier leaves this mining country, which bears misfortune in its genes.

The cut negatives for *Germinal* were delivered on June 9, 1913, and the film was released on October 4, 1913. The advertising referred to "Emile Zola's masterpiece" and mentioned the presence of Henry-Krauss, "the unforgettable Jean Valjean of *Les Misérables*." There was still no mention of the film's director, who remained unknown.

The movie was distributed in the United States in January 1914. As always with European movies at the time, it was cut by 3,000 feet (about 900 meters). But the reviewers still raved. "Gripping, forceful, pathetic and wonderfully realistic," said one. "In brief, that describes *Germinal,* a five-part picture, shortly on the General Film program. . . . So realistic is the picture that a person viewing it forgets that the principals are merely actors."[5] Another stated, "The good old word 'masterpiece' has been so foully abused by the press agents that he who wants to confine words to their proper meaning is tempted to hesitate in employing the word at all. No question of the appropriateness of the great word arises when applied to *Germinal.* It is in the true sense of the word a 'masterpiece.'"[6]

7

End of Reel

The year 1914 saw the last great SCAGL productions before the start of the Great War, a conflict that would shatter forever Capellani's life and that of his colleagues. At the time, Capellani was working on adaptations of two novels that took place during the French Revolution.

Capellani started filming *Le Chevalier de Maison-Rouge,* after a novel by Alexandre Dumas *père,* in autumn 1913, and the full negative was delivered on November 14. This 2,250-meter movie, released on February 27, 1914, was less adventurous than *Germinal.* It had the classic plot of a serial, with twists and turns. In fact, the film was similar to Louis Feuillade's serials produced at Gaumont, but the Capellani film was a costume drama. For this movie, the cast was unusually distinguished, with famous actors from the Paris stage; and this fact would be the main topic of the press campaign. Paul Escoffier, from the Theatre Antoine, played the title role; Marie-Louise Derval, from the Sarah Bernhardt Theatre, played Geneviève Dixmer; Léa Piron, from the Paris Opera, played Marie-Antoinette. The cast was enormous, and for once even the smaller parts were credited.

The film combined locations and studio sets less successfully than *Germinal.* The transitions were more abrupt, more noticeable. Dumas's story takes us to revolutionary Paris, where Royalists are trying to help Marie-Antoinette escape from her prison. The end of Dumas's novel is tragic, but the film supplies a happy ending. It must be said that the viewer cares less about the fate of the characters in this film than in *Germinal. Le Chevalier de Maison-Rouge* is more ordinary in its conception.

In July 1914, SCAGL began production on its adaptation of Victor Hugo's *Quatre-vingt-treize*. This vision of the Terror was a masterpiece. It's obvious Capellani was totally captivated by the three masterly characters created by Hugo. The Marquess of Lantenac (Philippe Garnier) is a hard-liner who ends up leading the Royalist movement; his nephew Gauvain (Paul Capellani) discovers the writings of Jean-Jacques Rousseau and becomes a soldier of the Revolution. And there is the magnificent Cirmourdain (Henry-Krauss), a simple country priest expelled from his parish because of his noble revolutionary ideals.

The film was a dazzling achievement, managing to render tangible the moral dilemmas of all three men. Should we always obey orders blindly? Should we treat an enemy with humanity even if that man would not hesitate to kill us in the same situation? Gauvain proves to be the most humane of the lot. He spares the life of a nun, in spite of the fact that she warned the Royalists of the presence of him and his group. In the same way, he asks that a man who had tried to kill him be well treated. The Marquess of Lantenac is the least prone to doubt. He could have a man or a woman who failed their commitment killed without emotion. We could think him totally insensitive until the end, when he suddenly shows another side to his personality. He turns back to spare the life of three innocent children. Cirmourdain, too, is a fanatic, following unfailingly the revolutionary precepts and frequently using the guillotine. Nevertheless, in the last scene he must face his own conscience. We must single out yet another extraordinary performance by Henry-Krauss, who played Cimourdain. Paul Capellani, too, showed his range in creating a masterful Gauvain, mixing elegance and panache.

Some sequences were obviously shot in Brittany (we can recognize the Mont-Saint-Michel bay in one sequence), while others were re-creations shot in a quarry near Maison-Alfort, a suburb southeast of Paris. To shoot the fire in La Tourgue tower, the filmmakers needed a plot of land away from their factory, which handled flammable film stock and houses. Vincennes therefore was not suitable. They decided to carry their wooden panels for the set to the quarry. The morning after their arrival, at 7:00 a.m., everybody, including around a hundred extras, was ready to shoot. Pierre Trimbach remembered what happened then. At 11:00 a.m., Capellani arrived in a taxi and told everybody the shooting was over; general mobilization had been declared. "There was a long silence," recalled Trimbach. "Nobody wanted to believe it, as we all wished so much that things would get better. We were motionless, looking at each other in silence. Suddenly, as if we were moved by a spring, the extras started singing 'La Marseillaise.' From the funnel-shaped quarry like a megaphone, 'La Marseillaise' flew over the countryside. Then, sadly, we went back to our cars and left La Tourgue tower still surrounded by smoke from the fighting. . . . In the car that brought us back to Vincennes, a performer was crying silently. She had an only son who was going, as well as her husband."[1]

Capellani later recalled that he was about to send Cimourdain to the guillotine when church bells started to sound the tocsin announcing general mobilization for the war.[2] Though confused about the character being executed, he may well have been shooting such a scene while the attack of La Tourgue was being prepared in Maison-Alfort. In any case, once the announcement was made, work stopped in the studio. The power was cut on August 18, and all activities ceased. The whole staff was mobilized. As for *Quatre-vingt-treize,* the film would only be released seven years later.

André Antoine is always mentioned as the person who finished the shooting of *Quatre-vingt-treize.* In fact, there is no tangible proof that he did so. André-Paul Antoine, Antoine's son, says in his book of memoirs that his father finished the film, giving no details.[3] Yet during the war André-Paul was at the front and did not know what his father was doing at the studio. As for other details, the surviving SCAGL register of correspondence for the period unfortunately does not mention anywhere the cost of *Quatre-vingt-treize*. There is only a small bill of 53 francs on September 25, 1917, without any reference. Such a small sum could not pay for a day of shooting. And if there were more sequences to shoot, all the actors would have had to be called back for such a purpose. Paul Capellani left for the United States in 1915 and did not return to France until 1919. If Antoine had made such a major contribution to the film, he would, without a shadow of a doubt, have asked to be mentioned in the credits when the film came out in 1921. He was asked to write an article for *Cinémagazine* about the censorship suffered by *Quatre-vingt-treize* during the war, yet he did not mention in the article any contribution he may have made to the film.[4] When in 1920 Antoine was working on *L'Arlésienne* (1922), Pierre Decourcelle asked him if he would agree to share director's credit with Georges Denola. Antoine replied very firmly in the negative, and Denola was downgraded to assistant director. This is yet more evidence that Antoine would not have agreed to be eliminated from the credits of a film he had participated in. In addition, there is no mention of *Quatre-vingt-treize* in the surviving correspondence between Decourcelle and Antoine.

Various versions of the Alexandre Arnoux script have been preserved. They show that Capellani modified some episodes considerably, particularly at the end of the film. While the movie concludes with Cimourdain's suicide, the different versions of the script all end with his death fighting the Royalists. As for the film's opening, it shows us the first meeting between Gauvain and Cimourdain, while the priest is still active in his parish. There was no such scene in Arnoux's script. Capellani's input into the script was therefore extremely important.

8

On the Front Line

General mobilization affected the three Capellani brothers. Albert, Paul, and Maurice all entered the army at the same time around the start of the war. In 1907, Maurice had joined the College Sainte-Barbe with a scholarship. He left the college in 1909 and was received with the rank of fifteen out of sixty in the Germain Pilon art school, in training to become a draftsman. On April 28, 1913, following his elder brothers' example, he signed up for three years in the army. Paul Capellani acted as a kind of foster father for his younger brother during his schooling. When the war started, Paul's was a famous name on the Paris stage, and he was on the verge of joining the most prestigious theater in France, La Comédie Française, when he entered the army in early August 1914. We can imagine Valérie-Anna Capellani's anguish to see her three sons leaving for the front line.

When I started researching Capellani, I had no information about his activities during the war period apart from what had been published in the American press. One of these sources mentioned that Albert had been an officer and "was relieved from duty through illness contracted at the battle of Soissons."[1] Actually, this was a distortion of reality: Capellani never was an officer, and he never fought near Soissons. Another article said he had "contracted a form of rheumatism that rendered him unfit for further service."[2] Here, too, the truth was different.

Albert Capellani joined his regiment—the 13th Territorial Army artillery regiment based in Vincennes—on August 3, 1914. He had the rank of corporal and would always remain a noncommissioned officer. The regiment left for the Meuse in the East of France on August 7 with 1,463 troops and 1,500 horses. The first weeks of the war involved rapid troop movements, with the Germans attacking and progressing rapidly across the north of France after invading Belgium, while the French regiments were posted along the German border. Trench warfare is nowadays so symbolic of the First World War that we almost forget those first weeks, which were different in nature and were incredibly costly in terms of human lives. André Antoine's son, André-Paul Antoine, recalled those first weeks at the front as complete disorganization. His regiment was decimated, and the front line moved so quickly he was completely lost.

Albert's regiment was positioned near the Luxemburg border. With the sudden German breakthrough, which threatened to encircle them, he and his comrades retreated across the Argonne. On October 1, Albert was promoted to the rank of sergeant. His military record gives no details regarding any injury. However, it is perfectly possible he could have been wounded, being in an artillery regiment on the front line. In any case, he must have been in a military hospital in December 1914 when a doctor diagnosed the chronic and incurable disease he suffered from: Albert was diabetic. Wounds do not heal easily with such a disease. An army doctor may have measured the glucose in his patient's urine when he noticed how slowly Albert's wounds were healing. Albert was then forty years old, and he had the perfect profile for adult-onset diabetes. He was rather portly and must have loved his food. His diabetes was acquired, not genetic. In the 1910s, the disease was known and could be diagnosed. But there was no cure. A doctor could only suggest a very strict diet, eliminating any trace of glucose. Given this diagnosis, Albert was discharged from military duty on December 19, 1914. This was confirmed on November 26, 1915, at the French consulate in New York with the following details: "Severe diabetes (4.8 grams of sugar per liter), albumin and kidney cells [in urine], and parenchymal nephritis." This report showed that Albert was already suffering from kidney failure. In those days, doctors were unable to measure blood glucose level. Nevertheless, the indication given by urine glucose level was still significant. For Capellani, it would have been out of the question to reveal his disease, as it could have severely handicapped his career.

His mother, Valérie-Anna, waited for news from her three sons. In October 1914, she had heard nothing from the youngest, Maurice. She sent a few lines to be published in the daily *Petit Parisien* in a section dedicated to families looking for news from their loved ones. These few lines betrayed her anguish: "Mrs. Capellani, 44 rue de Moscou, Paris, grateful to anybody who could give her news of Maurice Capellani, private in 72nd infantry regiment, 11th company, who has sent no letter for a month. Cable or write, cost of shipping refunded. Urgent."[3]

She did not know that her son had been dead for a month. Maurice Capellani was in Champagne near Maurupt when the Marne offensive was launched. On September 6, 1914, he was mortally wounded while his section was repelling a German attack. He received posthumously the Croix de Guerre, bronze star. He was only twenty.

Paul Capellani also joined his army corps on August 2, 1914. He belonged to the 24th section of military workers. His rank was sergeant. It is not known if he fought on the front line. He seems to have participated actively in boosting the morale of soldiers, giving theater performances in aid of charities. He was in Orléans in January 1915 when a draft board decided to keep him on active service. But on July 8, 1915, he was discharged by the same board for chronic gastritis. It is not known if he got his discharge by pulling strings. This seems unlikely, however, because at this time a whole generation was in uniform, whatever a young man's position on the social ladder.

At the beginning of 1915, Albert Capellani found himself

back in civilian life. He had to decide where his future lay. He was a filmmaker, but his studio was closed. He knew he suffered from an incurable disease, yet he could not dwell on it, as he had to provide for his family and three children.

9

Going or Staying

Since Albert's departure from SCAGL, the company had lain dormant, with its power cut off and its studio converted into soldiers' accommodations. Rumors were rife in the industry that the staff had not been paid what they were owed. According to Léon Gaumont, the rumor was that "the bankers closed the cash box and artists and other colleagues have not been paid!!"[1]

The head of SCAGL, Pierre Decourcelle, was participating in the war effort by managing a charity assisting military convalescents presided over by Countess Elisabeth Greffülhe.[2] In Bordeaux, in December 1914, he noted: "Gugenheim is in Paris, waiting for the moment to start work again usefully. It won't be easy: the performers, cameramen, extras, and workmen who make the prints are otherwise engaged. Yet we may manage to gather a small team for the beginning of spring."[3] Actually, Decourcelles had started negotiations with a famous theater director to persuade him to join SCAGL. As early as June 4, 1914, he wrote André Antoine: "We will soon be able to give you the answer we obtained from the Compagnie Générale Pathé, which will satisfy you entirely."[4]

If André Antoine was thinking of leaving the stage for the screen in 1914, the reasons were financial. He had accumulated a lot of debts and had no other resources. The challenge to move from the theater to the movie studio must have been also very exciting for him. He often came to watch the filming at SCAGL and must have developed an interest in motion pictures. From the point of view of the head of SCAGL, Decourcelle would certainly have liked to add such a famous name to his troupe of filmmakers. Until now the names of

SCAGL directors were not included in the company advertising, but that would change quickly in the next few years. Soon, even the portrait of some directors—such as Abel Gance, Henri Pouctal, and André Antoine—would appear at the opening of their feature films.

On April 9, 1915, Decourcelle told Antoine, "We wrote officially to the Compagnie Générale Pathé to ask permission to restart work. We are waiting for the reply, which will take time because they have to consult Mr. Pathé—currently in America."[5] Antoine was finally hired with a monthly salary of 1,200 francs. He trained inside the company with director Georges Denola, who taught him how to be a filmmaker. Yet Antoine noticed that the attitude toward him in the studio was rather nasty. A letter Antoine wrote to Decourcelle in early 1916 allows us to understand the situation inside Pathé as well as the reasons of Capellani's departure to America: "You must know I am aware that my arrival in moving pictures was like a stone in a frog pond. And from all sides I was made aware—even by anonymous letters—that it won't go like a dream. Before his departure, Capellani told several people, who repeated it to me, that my arrival prompted his departure. All this is rather unimportant and doesn't frighten me. What is more important is to state the conditions—from the beginning—in which, in my opinion, a devoted collaboration can produce what you expect."[6]

If there was any doubt left regarding the relationship between Antoine and Capellani, this letter shows they were not close friends and had no former link as mentor and pupil. After his discharge, Capellani was certainly thinking of returning to SCAGL; however, the arrival of a famous director put him in an awkward position. He would not have been able to exercise his authority as artistic director in those conditions. He certainly must have felt betrayed when he discovered that Decourcelle had hired Antoine in his absence. In addition, Capellani must have been really loved by his crew if some of them could show such hostility towards Antoine. The problem with Antoine was that he arrived to lord it over everyone, ready to revolutionize an art he still had not mastered. The technicians would have spotted his failings very quickly.

The news of Capellani's availability reached Léon Gaumont; news traveled fast in the industry. Gaumont decided at once to hire Capellani. The producer knew the quality of Capellani's work at a time when his own studio had been decimated because of the war. His artistic director, Louis Feuillade, had been mobilized, and he had to make do with less talented directors. Before asking Capellani directly, Gaumont sent a letter to Feuillade to ask for his opinion. "Cappellani [*sic*] is among the jobless. Do you see any drawbacks you want to express in case I start talking to him? Your departure will leave us very deprived. And I must find new directors, at least provisionally. [Gaston] Ravel's and [Maurice] Mariaud's productions are inadequate in terms of quality. And [Léonce] Perret cannot provide the main feature of each program all by himself."[7] This letter shows the standing of Capellani within the profession of the time.

Feuillade was probably a bit worried at the idea of having such a rival among his colleagues. Two artistic directors under the same roof? That was one too many. So his reply to Gaumont was cautious: "Capellani—Excellent director, but I do not think he can produce his own scripts. At SCAGL, he was making only adaptations. He would be a good collaborator if he was given screenplays. That's my impression anyway."[8] In the end, Gaumont gave up the idea. In any case, by the time Feuillade wrote this letter, Albert Capellani had already crossed the Atlantic Ocean.

Capellani realized that the American film industry would be interested in his talent. While the French industry was in severe decline due to lack of money and staff, on the other side of the Atlantic the motion picture industry was booming, in fact on its way to becoming a major US industry. Motion pictures were also undergoing a metamorphosis. Charles Pathé noticed how film grammar was evolving in America. In July 1916, he asked Pierre Decourcelle to modify the editing of SCAGL films. From now on, he wanted his films to follow the latest American innovations: to include close-ups systematically and to have shorter sequences with faster editing.

In America, the movie industry was very fond of French technicians and French directors, who could bring their own expertise to motion pictures. Thus, in May 1914 Maurice Tourneur had arrived in New York to direct the American subsidiary of Éclair. There was already a small colony of French people in the United States—directors Alice Guy-Blaché and Emile Chautard and cameramen René Guissart, Lucien Andriot, and Georges Benoit.

Capellani decided to try his luck across the pond. After all, *Les Misérables* and *Germinal* were both celebrated as masterpieces in America, even if his name was never mentioned. But things were about to change.

10

The Visualizer of
Les Misérables

On March 13, 1915, Albert Capellani boarded the SS *La Touraine* in Le Havre and arrived in New York on March 22. He was alone; he had left his family in Saint-Mandé. He was not crossing the Atlantic unprepared. He arrived with recommendations for Jules Brulatour at the Peerless Feature Producing Company. This was the contact name he gave the immigration officer at Ellis Island. Brulatour was an important, but shadowy, figure in the film industry of the time. He was not a producer in the true sense of the word, even though he provided funds for film production. He had worked as an agent for Eastman Kodak since 1911, amassing a fortune as he received a percentage on all sales of Kodak film stock. He used part of this money to invest in film production as a silent partner.

Capellani's first steps in America led him to the French consulate-general in New York, where he would record his new address. His military discharge was not yet permanent, and he had to state where he was living in case he was recalled. On March 23, he told the consulate that he was staying at the Theresa Hotel in Harlem at 125th Street and Seventh Avenue.

We can imagine the culture shock for a Frenchman arriving in New York for the first time in 1915. Capellani later recalled an intriguing anecdote. "When I came to this country," he said, "one of the first things I did after landing from my ship was to ride in the subway. Then the first thing that struck me on looking at the people around me was the number of them that were chewing gum. I had a friend with me, and I asked him the cause of this. He told me that the reason so many Americans chewed gum was that the pepsin was good for their stomachs. I wondered what was the matter with the American stomach and asked my friend. He said that many Americans suffered from indigestion because they eat too quickly, they did not give themselves enough time to digest their food. They rush through their breakfast, rush to the subway, rush through their lunch, and then at the end of the day rush home again. Their lives are one mad rush, so they chew gum for relief."[1]

Albert Capellani's arrival in the United States was soon mentioned in the trade press. As early as April 1915, we read, "The man who made *Les Misérables* joins World Film staff of directors."[2] Even a fan magazine noted his arrival: "Albert Capellani, the great French director, who photo-dramatized Victor Hugo's terrible master-thrust of realism, *Les Misérables,* is a recent addition to the direction staff of the World Film Corporation."[3] If Capellani's name appeared so rapidly, it must have had something to do with Brulatour, who was trying to promote the new recruit for the company he financed.

When Capellani arrived in March 1915, the American film industry was at a turning point. With America neutral in the war, the country's motion picture industry was booming. A multitude of small independent companies were born, started production, and died after a few years. But creativity was in full swing. The greatest event of the year had been the premiere of *The Birth of a Nation* in February 1915. D. W. Griffith's epic brought a fortune to theater exhibitors and to its director-producer, in spite of its enormous length—twelve reels. Mary Pickford was number one at the box office in 1915, making no fewer than eight features. Charlie Chaplin had only been working in motion pictures for a year; but he was already earning $1,250 a week with his new contract at Essanay, having started at Keystone in 1914 with a miserly $150 a week. The star system was already well established.

Competition and emulation were favored with a multitude of film companies, such as Vitagraph, Essanay, Lubin, Kalem, Selig, Universal, Pathé-Exchange, Mutual, and Triangle. If Pathé was concentrating on serials and others on two-reelers, the five-reel picture was nevertheless becoming the norm.

In February 1914, the World Film Corporation had been created. It was born of the combined forces of J. J. Shubert, a Broadway producer; William A. Brady, a theater producer; Arthur Spiegel, who owned a mail order house; and Lewis J. Selznick, a former jeweler. World Film already employed two French directors, Maurice Tourneur and Emile Chautard. The company studio was situated in Fort Lee, New Jersey. Motion picture production on the East Coast was concentrated in this small town, close enough to New York to be accessible by ferry across the Hudson River. Fort Lee offered enough space to build large studios, which looked like vast greenhouses; and it also afforded the possibility for filmmakers to shoot on location in the surrounding area. In 1915, film production in the East was still important, even if Hollywood was already providing 50 percent of the total film production in the United States.

Capellani realized he needed to adapt to his new environment, and to a new way of making movies. He spoke some English, thanks to his stay in London in 1898; he was therefore able to understand that American culture was completely different from the French. He also discerned that motion picture production in the United States was organized along the lines of the mass production system used in factories. Capellani observed that "when I arrived there [in the United States], like all Frenchmen who come out of his land for the first time, I thought I was a genius. I received quickly a strong lesson in humility when I realized that, after all, I knew nothing at all. I had to forget everything I knew and thought was the right way to learn my trade."[4]

With a new contract in hand, Capellani could now tell his wife and three children to join him. He also asked his wife to bring his large library of reference books. Léonie-Marie took the SS *Rochambeau* in Bordeaux on May 2, 1915, with Roger (aged ten), Simonne (seven), and Odette (three). Five days later, the RMS *Lusitania* was sunk by a German submarine off the coast of Ireland, creating an outcry in neutral America. Knowing his loved ones were still at sea, Capellani was so worried he was unable to work until his family arrived safely in New York. On May 12, the whole family was reunited; the trade papers reported the event.[5]

Albert's brother Paul and his mother were still in France. After his discharge on July 8, Paul obtained an authorization from the military authorities to go to the United States for three months as of August 1. With his mother, Valérie-Anna, Paul left Bordeaux on the SS *Chicago* on September 6. They arrived safely in New York on September 16. The trade press mentioned the actor's arrival: "[Paul] Capellani, one of the leading members of the Comédie Française Paris Stock Company, [and] a brother of Director Capellani, has just arrived from France on the French liner *Chicago*. M. Capellani is to be associated with the French theatre in the city during the coming season."[6] In fact, Paul did not come to work on the stage. During the entire period of the war, he would work in motion pictures. At the end of October, he was hired by the World Film Corporation and was going to work with his brother.

Le Chemineau (1905), an adaptation of the second chapter of Hugo's *Les Misérables*, one of Capellani's first films. (Fondation Jérôme Seydoux-Pathé)

La Légende de Polichinelle (1907). Polichinelle (Max Linder) surrounded by dwarfs in front of Pierrefonds castle. (Fondation Jérôme Seydoux-Pathé)

L'Arlésienne (1908). Second meeting between Frédéric and the Arlésienne. Capellani's first SCAGL production. (Fondation Jérôme Seydoux-Pathé)

Les Misérables (1912). Fantine (Marie Ventura) toils under the watchful eye of Jean Valjean (Henry-Krauss). (Fondation Jérôme Seydoux-Pathé)

Germinal (1913). Etienne Lantier (Henry-Krauss) arrives at the Monsou pit and meets old Bonnemort (Marc Gérard). (Fondation Jérôme Seydoux-Pathé)

Germinal (1913). Etienne Lantier (Henry-Krauss) has a bite to eat with Catherine Maheu (Sylvie) at the bottom of the mine. (Fondation Jérôme Seydoux-Pathé)

La Glu (1913). Fernande, aka "La Glu" (Mistinguett), devours fisherman Marie-Pierre (Paul Capellani) with her eyes. (Fondation Jérôme Seydoux-Pathé)

Le Chevalier de Maison-Rouge (1914). Marie-Antoinette (Léa Piron) at the Temple prison. (Fondation Jérôme Seydoux-Pathé)

Quatre-vingt-treize (1914). A superb portrait of Paul Capellani as Gauvain. (Lenny Borger Collection)

Capellani portrait inscribed to Lucien Andriot: "To my dear old Lucien, in friendly memory of a good year spent together which we will both remember . . . I hope.—April 24, 1916." (Dominique Lebrun Collection)

The World Film Company directors and stars in 1915. Seated, left to right: Dorothy Fairchild, Wilton Lackaye, Elaine Hammerstein; standing, left to right: Albert Capellani, Frank Crane, Emile Chautard, Holbrook Blinn, Maurice Tourneur, Alice Brady, James Young, Clara Kimball Young. (Dominique Lebrun Collection)

The set for *Camille* (1915), with Albert Capellani and art director Ben Carré in the center, reclining on furniture. (Dominique Lebrun Collection)

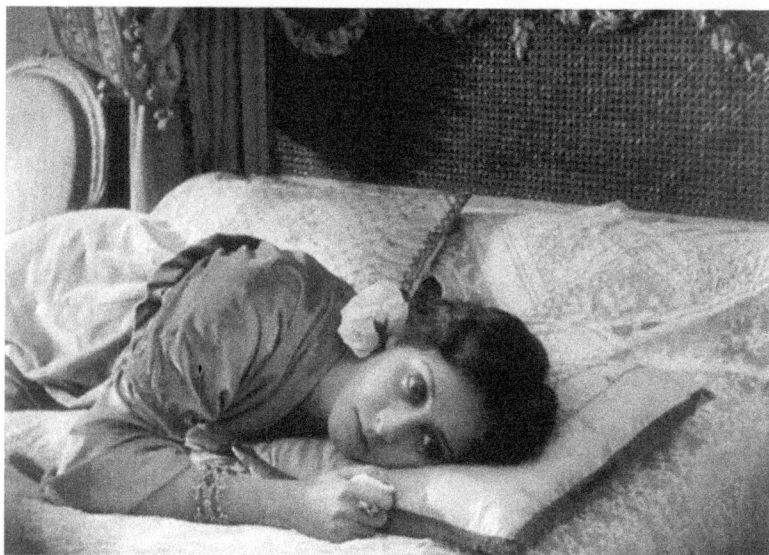

Camille (1915). Clara Kimball Young as Marguerite Gautier. (Národní filmový archiv)

The Feast of Life (1916). Robert Frazer, Paul Capellani, and Clara Kimball Young. (Archive.org)

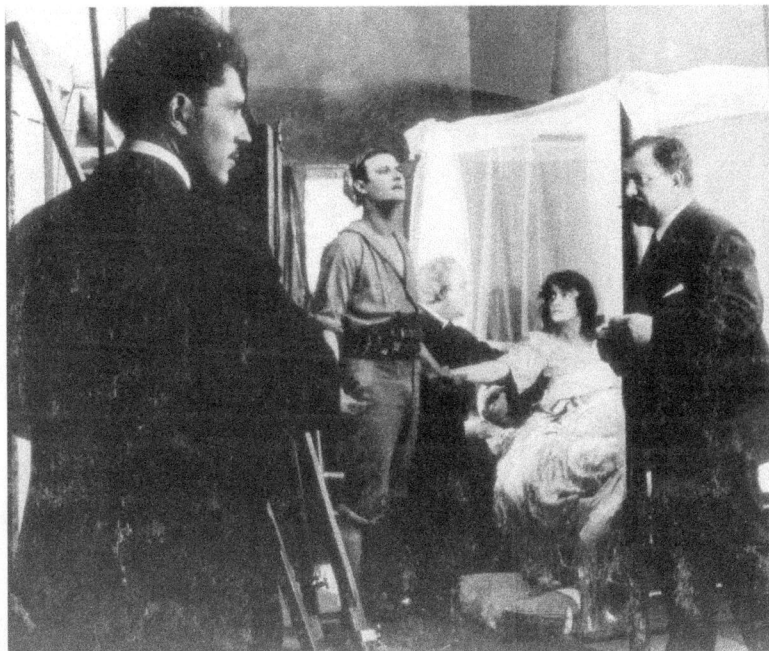

Left to right: Cameraman Lucien Andriot, Robert Frazer, Edward M. Kimball, Doris Kenyon, and Albert Capellani on the set of *The Feast of Life* (1916). (Dominique Lebrun Collection)

On the set of *The Feast of Life* at the Paragon studio. Capellani is seated in the center; standing on his right, Lucien Andriot; seated on the table, art director Ben Carré. (Dominique Lebrun Collection)

The set of *La Vie de Bohème* (1916). Albert Capellani in the center with his brother Paul seated beside him and Lucien Andriot holding the camera. (Dominique Lebrun Collection)

Cameraman Lucien Andriot and Albert Capellani under the snow in Fort Lee, New Jersey, circa 1916. (Dominique Lebrun Collection)

Lakewood, O. 12/6/16.

Mr. Paul Capellani,
c/o C Young Picture Studio,
New York City,N.Y.

Dear Sir:--

　　　　　I take off my hat to you as the most
excellent and versatile film performer in the
world.
　　　　　After having seen you a number of
times, in your many splendid plays, most of
them so true to life, I beg leave to thank you
very much for the pleasure and entertainment
given me and also wish you the success of many
more years to come, and also hope to see you
many more times.
　　　　　Although I have never met you nor
shakened your hand, I wish to ask you, if you
should ever stop in Cleveland to make a visit
to please advertise it a little before time, so
that many of your Cleveland admirers may have
the pleasure of seeing the man ,who has tried
his best to please the criticising public and
has so splendidly succeeded, may his fame be
everlasting!
　　　　　I should highly appreciate it if you
would send me your photo with your autograph
upon it.
　　　　　I think that I have taken up enough
of your very valuable time and will close now
with again wishing you the success of many more
years to come, and hoping to hear from you in the
near future and also thanking you in advance for
any favours you may extend to me, I beg to remain,
　　　　　　　　　Respectfully yours,

　　　　　　　　　D.Ahlgrimm,
1274 Fry St Lakewood, O.

An American fan letter to Paul Capellani, December 6, 1916 (see Chapter 12). (Bernard Basset-Capellani Collection)

CHRISTOPHER COLUMBUS and COUNT ZEPPELIN

WERE MY SILENT PARTNERS IN THE

CLARA KIMBALL YOUNG

FILM CORPORATION

At first thought you say—"That's Impossible."

But that has been the world's FIRST thought on EVERY extraordinary stunt, including the discovery of America and the conquest of the air.

Things that EVERYBODY believes possible aren't WORTH DOING.

The CLARA KIMBALL YOUNG FILM CORPORATION was considered "impossible."

And now, it is ALREADY the greatest success in the game, backed by five-year contracts with the most substantial theatre and exchange interests in the United States.

It's an all-round square deal—that's why it won out—Everybody from the star to the public gets the best of it.

BUT BEST OF ALL, IT SOUNDS THE DEATH KNELL OF THE PROGRAM SYSTEM.

Do you know what that means to YOU, Mr. and Mrs. and Miss Movie Fan?

It means the end of a system that forces you to see FIVE BAD PICTURES to one GOOD one.

At present the stars you admire most are used to club the exhibitor into line.

In order to get the pictures of YOUR FAVORITE STAR your theatre manager has to contract for all the other pictures produced by that star's company. The company makes the exhibitor take any sort of cheap, worthless features along with the one big picture turned out every five or six weeks.

That's what the PROGRAM SYSTEM has done to YOU!

This is what the CLARA KIMBALL YOUNG FILM CORPORATION has done to the PROGRAM SYSTEM.

It has pointed the way to OPEN BOOKING.

Beginning with the six-reel production of ROBERT W. CHAMBERS' epochal novel, "THE COMMON LAW," in October, and followed by "THE FOOLISH VIRGIN," from the pen of THOMAS DIXON, author of "THE BIRTH OF A NATION," all of MISS CLARA KIMBALL YOUNG'S pictures will be produced under the direction of that master of screencraft, ALBERT CAPELLANI, and distributed without connection with ANY PROGRAM OF ANY SORT.

In addition I shall present other prominent stars ON THE SAME PLAN.

The other producers will have to adopt my theories or GO TO THE WALL.

Soon you will be able to see ALL YOUR FAVORITE STARS under an OPEN DOOR policy that will send much of the present day film trash to the ash-barrel and put the motion picture on a plane with its allied arts—drama and music.

LEWIS J. SELZNICK,
PRESIDENT OF THE

CLARA KIMBALL YOUNG FILM CORPORATION

Advertisement for the Clara Kimball Young Film Corporation in *Variety*, July 21, 1916. (Archive.org)

Ad for *The Common Law* (1916). (Archive.org)

Left to right: Metro technical director Edward J. Shulter, assistant director Leander de Cordova, and Albert Capellani preparing *Social Hypocrites* (1918). (Dominique Lebrun Collection)

Alla Nazimova, author Edith Wherry, and Albert Capellani preparing *The Red Lantern* (1919). (Dominique Lebrun Collection)

Capellani preparing Nazimova for a wet scene in *Out of the Fog* (1919). (Dominique Lebrun Collection)

The Red Lantern (1919). Mrs. Ling (Margaret McWade) asks her granddaughter Mahlee (Alla Nazimova) to cut her feet. (Kevin Brownlow Collection)

The Red Lantern (1919). Mahlee (Alla Nazimova) and the statue of the Goddess of Peace, made by Victor Andre. (Kevin Brownlow Collection)

Cartoon of Capellani showing Dolores Cassinelli in *The Virtuous Model* (1919) how it should be done. "On my bended knees, I ask you to forgive!" he cries, while the cameraman looks on. (Archive.org)

Advertisement for *Oh, Boy!* (1919). (Archive.org)

Ad for *The Young Diana* (1922). (Archive.org)

Albert Capellani, seated under camera, directs Marion Davies in *The Young Diana* (1922), with cameraman Harold Westrom. (Dominique Lebrun Collection)

The Capellani family in Fort Lee. Left to right: Albert, Simonne, Roger, Odette, and Léonie-Marie. (Bernard Basset-Capellani Collection)

Left to right: Roger, Léonie-Marie, Albert, Odette, and Simonne Capellani. (Bernard Basset-Capellani Collection)

11

World Film Corporation

Albert Capellani found himself surrounded with fellow coun-
trymen at the World Film Corporation. The lead director of
the company was Maurice Tourneur. He had arrived in New
York on May 1, 1914, at the request of Charles Jourjon, the
head of the Éclair company. However, in February 1914, the
Éclair laboratory in Fort Lee had been destroyed by a fire.
Jourjon then decided to stop production under the Éclair banner and to promote a new company, called Peerless Feature
Producing, together with Jules Brulatour. A new studio was
erected near the previous Éclair one, and production started
there in November 1914. Tourneur was put in charge of the
new Peerless-World studios, where he would direct technically
innovative pictures whose lighting and artistic qualities would
make him famous in the film industry. *The Wishing Ring* (1914)
and *Alias Jimmy Valentine* (1915) showed pictorial and dramatic qualities, as well as a sense of humor, beyond those of
many contemporary American pictures. The studio employed
other Frenchmen as well, including cameraman Lucien Andriot
and set designers Ben Carré and Henri Ménessier. Director
Emile Chautard joined them later, in January 1915.

In his memoirs, Ben Carré told of his relationships with the
three French directors, in particular with Capellani. "Albert, a
portly bearded gentleman, was welcomed by everyone in the
Studio. He [came to be] called 'Cap' by the French clan and
myself, who used 'Mister' for Tourneur and 'Monsieur' for

Chautard; I didn't see anything wrong in calling him 'Cap' like the others."[1] Capellani was more friendly and informal than his colleagues. Tourneur had a strong temper and maintained a rather cool relationship with his staff, as his faithful assistant Clarence Brown recalled. Capellani was the only one to have an affectionate nickname. He was evidently informal in his professional relationships at SCAGL, and he felt in his element at the World studio. He noticed nevertheless that the work schedule was a lot heavier than in France. Everybody worked all day without a break, whatever their job. He also discovered teamwork, where each project was divided according to the Taylor management system: work in the studio was divided into various departments.

To get an idea of how movies were made at the time, we fortunately have a delightful comedy made by Maurice Tourneur entitled *A Girl's Folly* (1917). This picture was produced at the Paragon studio and shows us the side of moviemaking behind the camera. Doris Kenyon plays a romantic and naïve country girl who follows a movie actor (Robert Warwick) to Fort Lee in the hope of becoming a film star. Tourneur shows us every aspect of the studio, with the staff arriving in the morning, the canteen, and the studio sets. Film stars arrive in the morning without any idea of what the script contains. They put on their makeup themselves, and the director sketches the scene they are about to play. The set is constructed rapidly. Some wooden frames are fitted together to create the walls of the room and are placed on a wooden revolving platform. This way, the studio hands just need to rotate the wooden base to get the set lit properly by the sun. The whole studio resembles a giant greenhouse, where several directors are working at the same time. The cameraman cranks steadily, and when the scene is done, a still photographer comes over to shoot the actors overacting with gusto the western sequence they have just performed.[2] Here Tourneur and his screenwriter, Frances Marion, have added a touch of humor to the proceedings: unlike what is shown in the film, we know that Tourneur was not the kind of director who liked his actors unprepared. Tourneur himself appears briefly in his shirtsleeves in two scenes of his film.

Capellani started working just two months after his arrival in the United States. In May 1915, he made his first American feature, *The Face in the Moonlight* (1915), with Robert Warwick in the lead dual role; Warwick was then one of the main World Film stars. The picture takes place during the French Restoration (that is, the reign of Louis XVIII), while conspirators are trying to reinstate Napoléon to the throne. Two half-brothers, who look so much alike as to be twins, are on opposite sides: one is a blue-blooded officer of the King, while the other is a criminal. The aristocrat ends up being accused of the crime committed by his half-brother. Capellani seemed to be having fun on the set: a publicity shot shows him standing beside the guillotine with a small black cat on his left shoulder as he looks at Robert Warwick, who is lying on the plank, ready to be beheaded. Capellani considered a black cat as a mascot and had one in all his films. The film was shot at the new Peerless-World studio, and Capellani took advantage of the new outdoor stage to escape the stifling heat of the glass studio. In one sequence, Warwick appears in backlit silhouette against the moonlight. This inspired Ben Carré, Maurice Tourneur, and Robert Warwick to organize an informal competition to find out who had the longest nose. Ben Carré was delighted to be a lucky loser! The film was praised in the press; one journal noted that "Albert Capellani was an ideal choice for director of this five-part World Film drama with Robert Warwick in a dual role. . . . From first to last, the picture reveals the guidance of a man thoroughly versed in the subject and a master of photoplay production. The settings and furnishings of the rooms were selected with a keen eye for artistic results, frequently scenes were photographed from an unexpected angle, gaining effects at once pleasing and novel. . . . Nor is it surprising that he has imparted the spirit of a French romance with a completeness seldom to be expected of an American company working in an American studio."[3] As usual, however, *Variety* was rather scathing in its comments: "The piece was a poor selection for a film unless the scenario adapter fell down. Certainly someone flopped with it. It could never help any service program."[4]

Capellani took no rest. That July, he was shooting *The Impostor* (1915) at the Peerless-World studio, again with Lucien Andriot as cameraman. The company traveled to Pittsburgh to film some scenes on location. The film received a mixed press; a typical notice read, "Had the adaptation of the play been more carefully arranged the faultiness of the picture version would be in a large measure alleviated."[5]

In August, Capellani was casting his third film, *The Flash of an Emerald* (1915). If his first two American features did not seem to contain any novel technical features, this third film was, by contrast, extremely intriguing because of its narrative structure. Robert Warwick plays the part of a gentleman crook along the lines of Arsène Lupin or Raffles. The film opens with a scene in director Capellani's office. Robert Warwick comes in, and Capellani asks him (in a title card): "How would you like to play a wicked villain?" Warwick flatly refuses, but finally agrees to read the script. The film-within-the-film then starts as he reads. At the end, we find Warwick again in Capellani's office. He throws down the script on his desk and exclaims, "I wouldn't play this contemptible scoundrel for $10,000!" This film-within-the-film structure was quite novel for the time. Mauritz Stiller was the only other director to use such an idea, in *Vingarna* (1916), where he appeared as himself, making screen tests with Nils Asther before selecting Lars Hanson for the lead of his next film. This technique was also for Capellani a device to allow his lead actor to play against type. As he had done on his previous film, Capellani went on location, this time to Sainte-Anne-de-Beaupré in Canada to film a famous religious pilgrimage, which is included in his picture. Unfortunately, only one reel of *The Flash of an Emerald* has survived, and it is awaiting restoration. The *Variety* reviewer seemed impressed by the picture's innovative aspect: "Intense suspensive interest well acted throughout and absolutely redeemed by the opening and closing, which saves Warwick's reputation as 'matinee idol.' Will do anywhere."[6]

Capellani's next film was going to be in a different class altogether. In October, the trade press mentioned a new production that was in preparation, with the new female star of the studio under Capellani's direction. The World Film Corporation managed to poach Clara Kimball Young, an actress who was previously under contract with Vitagraph. As screenwriter Frances Marion described her, Young was "a voluptuous brunette with large dark expressive eyes whose face in repose suggested a melancholy nature. Actually, she was effervescent as charged water [and] fun loving."[7] The man who organized Young's transfer to World was Lewis J. Selznick. This colorful character was then vice-president of the company. A former jeweler, Selznick had broken into the film industry like a burglar by appropriating an empty office at Universal. As vice-president of World Film, he was already thinking of taking his freedom from the big boss, William A. Brady. The relationship between the two men was tense. They were both self-made men with a temper. Born in San Francisco of Irish parentage, Brady started life as a butcher's boy. After several menial jobs, he became a major prizefight organizer and handled the career of James J. Corbett. Finally, he became one of Broadway's great names and managed the Playhouse theater, and also became the head of World, where he could use his large catalog of plays for film adaptations. As Capellani's production was being prepared, he was given a shy young girl to work with. Frances Marion was not yet the famous Oscar-winning screenwriter she became later. Before she was assigned to Capellani's film, she was given the unrewarding task of saving a picture with actress Alice Brady, who happened to be the boss's daughter.

Marion recalled humorously her first meeting with the explosive William A. Brady:

"I'm the writer you hired at two hundred dollars a week if I made good on my first job," the young screenwriter said.

"Two hundred dollars a week! Well, I'll be goddamned! Never heard of paying such a salary to a writer!"

"Neither did I. But it's about time the writers got on the gravy train."

"When I was a kid in San Francisco selling peanuts on a train I knew I was going places even then. What's the hell's your name?"

"Frances Marion."

"Sounds like the madam of a whorehouse. I'll call you Pete."[8]

Frances was put in charge of the script for Clara Kimball Young's next vehicle, a new version of *Camille*. Paul Capellani had been selected to play Armand Duval. The screenwriter was amused by Clara's reaction after reading the script: "Another one of those stinkpot stories. All I've got to do in this one is cough, kiss a Frenchie named Armand, then keep on coughing until I kick the bucket."[9] Her reaction was all the more amusing when contrasted with what was published in the press. Clara Kimball Young was said to have studied the effect of tuberculosis on its victims as preparation for playing Marguerite. She even allegedly went to visit a sanitarium in Saranac Lake, New York, to complete her study.[10]

Capellani's *Camille* is a genuine achievement. The story of the Lady of the Camellias has been updated, the film's first working title being *A Modern Camille*.[11] This idea of updating the story would be repeated for the version directed by R. C. Smallwood in 1921, with Alla Nazimova surrounded by Art

Nouveau sets, and also for the Fred Niblo version, produced in 1927 with Norma Talmadge, (over)decorated by William Cameron Menzies. Unlike those two later versions, Capellani avoided the ostentatious and the hyperbolic. He created a simple, yet refined version of the novel by Alexandre Dumas *fils*. The set and furniture are modest, depicting a middle-class home as it was at the time. Under Lucien Andriot's lighting, Marguerite meets Armand at an exhibition of paintings. Later, they meet again and fall in love. He then realizes she is kept by Count de Varville and develops an intense jealousy. In the end, Marguerite decides to leave Paris with Armand, and they go off to live in the country. But their idyll is shattered by Armand's father, who comes to ask Marguerite to leave his son in order to save the family's honor. After fighting a duel (a swordfight) with the count, Armand returns to a dying Marguerite.

What sets Capellani's film apart from the later versions of *Camille* is the attention to detail. Each character's position on the social ladder is carefully depicted. Also, unlike the other versions, Marguerite explains how she became a kept woman, pocketing checks from elderly gentlemen. In a long flashback, she explains to Armand what her life has been. As a child, she lived in a hovel with her mother, who asked her to sweep the floor like little Cosette. Later, as a young girl, she worked as a seamstress in a workshop where a supervisor tried to take advantage of her. She slapped his face and was fired. She ended up in the street, under the snow like Fantine, with nowhere to go. This description of Marguerite's background gives the character far more depth and allows the viewer to better understand her. Similarly, Marguerite's friends are also shown as three-dimensional characters, with their greed and their failings. During the first meeting between Armand and Marguerite, we observe Prudence and Gaston, who are stuffing themselves with food, completely indifferent to the discomfort of their hostess. Capellani uses an elegant panoramic shot to show us those two freeloaders.

Clara Kimball Young had just played *Trilby* (1915) under Maurice Tourneur's direction; in that film she showed her skills at characterization, playing a young working-class model who becomes an opera singer thanks to the power of the terrifying Svengali. Even if Young's healthy figure was not quite right for Marguerite Gautier, she managed to give the character charm and sincerity. Her death scene is excellent. Positioned by a fireplace as she awaits Armand's return, the flames provide a beautiful chiaroscuro. Her maid, backlit, opens the window that Marguerite might watch for Armand. Young's pairing with Paul Capellani is quite successful; they remain attractive to a modern audience.

Paul Capellani had lost weight since the shooting of *Quatre-vingt-treize*. He also had shaved his moustache, and American women fell for his elegant and lean figure. His Armand is more mature and surer of himself than the young actors usually selected for the part. (Paul was thirty-eight, but did not look it.) Paul was a versatile actor who did not limit himself to romantic leads. His impact on the audience was immediate. As one review noted, "In the first reel you may not like young Capellani. That's because not only he but his style is genuinely new. In the last act you'll be a Capellani enthusiast."[12]

Immediately following the film's release, Paul Capellani began to receive fan letters; thus was the power of motion pictures. He must have been impressed by his fans' reactions, as he kept some of their letters. Some were written on small cards. Here is one:

Kansas City, Mo.
March 5th, 1916

Mr. Paul Cappelani [*sic*]
World Film Corporation
Fort Lee, N.J.

Dear Mr. Cappelani [*sic*],

Just this evening I saw you with Clara Kimball Young in "Camille." Miss Young is very beautiful and plays Camille so very well. But it is in you that I see something decidedly new in leading-man-ship. Your acting is so clean-cut and finished.

Will you tell me the name of a play you can be seen in again soon?

I, too, am an actress, trying to come up in the usual manner. You will never meet me so won't you please send me your photo.

Sincerely,

2535 Forest Ave.   Miss Norma A. Mott[13]

Camille was released in December 1915 and was a success with both critics and audience. *Moving Picture World* noted, "The World Film Corporation was fortunate in securing a director of the French school, such as Albert Capellani, to produce this subject; also in casting Paul Capellani as Armand, and certainly both did much toward giving the drama a French atmosphere."[14] The reviewer for *Variety* also praised the actors: "The cast throughout is one of the best that has ever assembled for a picture. Paul Capellani (brother of Albert Capellani who directed the feature) plays Armand, and gives to it that indescribable touch so essential to the creation of the French atmosphere."[15]

World had by this time built a new studio, the Paragon, which offered better facilities and more capacity, and whose vice-president and general manager was Maurice Tourneur. In January 1916, Albert Capellani signed a new contract with Paragon. His salary was increased from $200 to $500 a week. According to *Variety*, a clause in his new contract specified "that there shall be no interference from anybody" in his work.[16] After the success of *Camille*, the studio decided to keep the same pair of stars, Clara Kimball Young and Paul Capellani, for a whole series of melodramas to be directed by Capellani. Their next feature was *The Feast of Life* (1916), written again by Frances Marion. She had moved up the ladder in the company and was now editor-in-chief of the scenario department. This story of bloody revenge could have easily turned into a silly melodrama of the worst kind. In fact, the picture is thrilling hokum in the mold of the runaway melodramas from the Golden Age of Hollywood. The film has the added bonus of being shot in Cuba. Capellani cleverly used numerous locations there, shot with the diligent care of Lucien Andriot, his favorite cameraman at the time. The story concerns the beautiful Aurora Fernandez (Clara Kimball Young), who has been forced against her will to marry the rich Don Armada (Paul Capellani, playing against type) in order to please her mother. As Aurora is on her way to church carrying a bunch of lilies, looking like a Madonna, a poor fisherman, Pedro (Robert Frazer), catches sight of her and is spellbound; he returns to the church that night to steal the flowers. Soon after, dressed as a country girl, Aurora goes to a tavern and meets Pedro. They flirt, but he doesn't realize she is the girl he is in love with. Meanwhile, Pedro's sister Celida (Doris Kenyon) has an adventure with Don Armada, who rejects her. She tries to commit suicide. Learning his sister's fate, Pedro decides to avenge her. He leads a group of fishermen to Armada's house and strikes him with a cutlass. Blinded, Armada collapses, though a doctor later manages to restore his sight. As Armada first glimpses the sunlight again, he discovers Aurora and Pedro in a tender embrace. Pretending still to be blind, Armada plots revenge. He arranges a meeting with Pedro and stabs him. He then returns home and tells Aurora of his crime. In despair, she struggles with him. Armada, whose wounds have not healed properly, collapses and dies. Pedro and Aurora are finally reunited.

Frances Marion used all the clichés of the worst melodramas in this screenplay, piling up every situation one can expect in such pictures. Nevertheless, the film remains coherent, thanks to the quality of its acting and of its cinematography. Paul Capellani, with his hair covered in gel and his virile moustache, is the perfect elegant villain. He created a violent and reckless hidalgo who stops at nothing to reach his goal. Squeezed into his Cuban-style clothes, he rides a horse with class. Clara Kimball Young, wrapped in a Spanish shawl, is a sensual Aurora. World's young leading lady, Doris Kenyon, who was also in Tourneur's *The Pawn of Fate* (1916) and *A Girl's Folly* (1917), plays her part with feeling. Lucien Andriot managed to capture the intense Cuban sunshine with some superb backlit sequences, and shot some remarkable indoor scenes as well, with light filtered through Venetian blinds. However, the hot Cuban climate seemed to have created problems. Several trade papers found fault with the cinematography. "Many of the Cuban scenes are overlighted," one noted, "and in some of the full pictures, the backgrounds are granulated and indistinct, faults probably caused by poor film."[17]

Critical reception was mixed. *Variety* found the film "well acted and directed and fine exterior locations, but the subject is cheap."[18] *Moving Picture World* noted that "unquestionably the first asset of *The Feast of Life* is Miss Young, whose playing lacks nothing in expressiveness and feeling; the second is a reasonably diverting story, and the third is in the appeal to the eye through unusual and picturesque locations, which, however, were not always clearly photographed."[19]

While the company was shooting in Cuba, the World Film Corporation underwent some radical changes of management.[20] At the beginning of February 1916, Lewis J. Selznick left World to create another production company of which he would be president and director general. Some sources suggest he was kicked out of World following a disagreement with William A. Brady. In any case, Brady never guessed Selznick's trump card. The cunning Lewis J. took with him World's main asset, Clara Kimball Young, the one star who was enabling

World Film to stay afloat. Clara seems to have been romantically involved with Selznick—for a short time. In any case, it was certainly part of Selznick's plan to keep her close to him. Brady was furious over this development and showed his exasperation toward Selznick in public during a meeting of exhibitors. From his tone, we can guess he would have liked to wring his former associate's neck. He warned exhibitors, "If you fellows allow every adventurer, grafter and pettifogger who controls the destiny of some star, made prominent by your efforts, to start a special company, raise the rental prices to three times what they are now, within the next three months every man at the head of a program will do the same thing and your service will cost you just four hundred per cent more than it is today."[21]

Young's contract at World ran until July. So, for the moment, she remained with the company. But Selznick had grand plans: to build a new studio for his star.

Capellani's next project was *La Vie de Bohème* (1916), with his compatriot Ben Carré as art director. Albert had earlier, in 1912, adapted Henri Murger's novel to the screen, with Suzanne Revonne and Paul Capellani in a 770-meter film entitled *La Bohème* (running about 35 minutes). A comparison between the two versions shows the giant leap in motion picture technique in the space of just four years. First of all, the mediocre painted Pathé backdrops in the earlier film are replaced by superb three-dimensional sets built by Carré. The 1916 picture is a five-reeler of more than 1,600 meters (about 70 minutes at 20 fps) and contains a mixture of close-ups, medium shots, and long shots instead of the usual long shot of 1912. Sequences are shorter in the US film, and the pacing is quicker. In both versions, Paul Capellani plays Rodolphe, the bohemian poet in love with Mimi. He had adapted perfectly to the new American technique of moviemaking. In the space of just a few months, he played Armand Duval, a dyed-in-the-wool villain, and Rodolphe—showing a remarkable versatility in an industry already in love with typecasting.

This *Vie de Bohème* is enchanting, due to Andriot's lighting effects and Carré's magnificent sets. The latter re-created Paris in the Paragon studio at Fort Lee that looked like the real thing. Each set was a little masterpiece: Rodolphe's attic room with its large window; the café where the bohemian artists gather, with its typical black-and-white tiled floor; and the banks of the Seine, with the traditional booksellers' boxes. Carré managed to capture a real Parisian atmosphere. He would also be in charge of the sets for the next adaptation of *La Bohème*, directed by King Vidor in 1926, with Lillian Gish and John Gilbert.

In the 1916 film, Mimi was played by Alice Brady, the daughter of the producer. According to some sources, she was the one who suggested adapting the novel after watching a performance of Puccini's opera at the Metropolitan Opera with Lina Cavalieri. For a modern film lover, Alice Brady is remembered for her performance in Gregory La Cava's *My Man Godfrey* (1936), in which she plays with flair Carole Lombard's eccentric mother. Twenty years earlier, however, the dimpled and round-faced Alice was an ingénue, and her Mimi is perfectly credible while being completely different from Lillian Gish's portrayal. We first discover Mimi as an orphan, abandoned at birth on the steps of a convent. After being raised by nuns, she becomes a servant to an innkeeper, who makes her work relentlessly. Exhausted, she leaves the place and starts making artificial flowers. This is how she meets Rodolphe, who is working, without enthusiasm, as secretary to his rich uncle. The bohemian life prevails, and he leaves his job to join a group of penniless artists. Mimi and Rodolphe end up as neighbors in the same building and on the same floor. Their romance starts as her candle has been blown out by a draft. Their love story is crushed by the old uncle, who tells Mimi that he wants Rodolphe to marry a woman he has selected for him. Mimi agrees to leave Rodolphe when his uncle begs her to. This reprise of *Camille* seems rather odd in *La Bohème*. Perhaps the producer, William A. Brady, asked screenwriter Frances Marion to make Mimi as pure as possible. In this telling, she leaves Rodolphe not because she wishes to have a better life, but out of self-sacrifice. Brady may not have been ready to see his daughter playing a loose woman. In any case, this small modification is of no importance, thanks to the stimulating performances of the actors. Paul Capellani shows another side of his talent as the penniless poet. The film opens with his awakening after a rough night. He protests when a servant enters and opens the curtain. He asks the servant to take away the clock. Then he starts looking for his shoes, which are lost somewhere in the room. Paul later said in an interview that Rodolphe was his favorite part. A captivated fan wrote him after seeing him in the film:

> 29 Red Rock Street, East Lynn, Massachusetts
> August 18, 1916
>
> My dear Mr. Capellani,
>   Not long ago I saw you in "La Vie de Bohème" and I enjoyed it so much. Your acting certainly is marvelous and I assure you that the only regret I have is that I do not see you enough.
>   I shall never forget the first time I saw you. It was in "Camille" with Miss Clara Kimball Young. How wonderful you were and I have always been most interested in your acting. I should love to see you in person—but never expect this good fortune. Now as long as I shall probably never see you—may I, please, have one of your autographed photos?
>   With my very best wishes to you.
>   I am most sincerely yours,
>
> E. A. Riefkohl[22]

La Vie de Bohème was released in June 1916 to unanimous applause. "Produced with rare taste to realize the full romantic value of Henri Murger's story and acted with intelligence and feelings, *La Vie de Bohème* occupies a certain place among five-part photoplays of the first class. It might well have been extended several reels, without running the risk of wearying an audience. . . . Atmospheric settings, artistic lighting and perfect photography play a considerable part in making the picture the exceptional example of screen art that it is," noted one review.[23] *Variety* wrote, "The altogether tragic life story of the little French foundling is admirably set forth in the film version of the story and the picture is practically one of the best that has been turned out by the World Corp. in some time."[24]

After four months' absence from the screen, Clara Kimball Young reappeared for the last time in a World production in September 1916, again under the direction of Capellani. *The Dark Silence* (1916) was a five-reel melodrama about love and jealousy between an English lord (Edward T. Langford) and a young doctor (Paul Capellani) who are both in love with the same volunteer nurse (Clara Kimball Young). For once, the Great War was mentioned in a Capellani picture. But it served only as the setting for a traditional love story. In the opinion of *Moving Picture World*, "The production of the picture is well done, except in a few incidences. The trench scenes could have been made more impressive, and one or two points in the plot should have been cleared up—notably, Mildred's marriage under a false name; but the grand climax with which the author rounds out his story, sweeps away all thought of any previous weakness of incident."[25]

The Dark Silence was the last picture at World Film for both actress and director. Clara's contract expired on July 15, and Capellani was appointed director general of the Clara Kimball Young Film Corporation. Lewis J. Selznick was now their boss.

12

Woman's Director

The relationship between Lewis J. Selznick and William A. Brady had always been difficult. For one thing, they had divergent views about casting. Brady thought that a good actor must and should play any kind of part. But Selznick believed a star had to create a certain image in the public's mind and stay with it. Frances Marion remembered one of their conversations about Doris Kenyon, a promising young actress in the studio.

> "What's more, I intend to guide Doris Kenyon's career along the route to fame," said Selznick.
> "Like hell you will!" the irate Irishman flashed back. "You can't wreck her career." Triumphantly, "I have a personal contract with Doris."
> Selznick outsnorted him. "I suppose you'll have her play a schoolteacher in one picture, an old chestnut vendor in another. Go ahead and waste all that beauty! You're getting too damned senile to appreciate it!"
> "Balls!" said Mr. Brady.
> "I accept it as a compliment," said Mr. Selznick.[1]

Besides their disagreements over casting, Selznick's new plans to rent Clara Kimball Young's films at a higher price seemed totally foolish to Brady. When the latter attacked his rival in front of exhibitors, saying his gamble would not pay off, Selznick seemed very sure of himself when he replied, "It is true that they had Clara Kimball Young in the past for pictures at $25 a day, but Miss Young carried the remainder of the program which was inferior to her features. I wish to go on record as saying that if, in the future, any exhibitor finds he does not make more money with Miss Young's pictures at $100 a day than he did when he paid $25, I stand ready to fund him his rental charge. I am willing to assume the entire gamble."[2]

Selznick implemented his program with Clara. From now on, she had to be mysterious and elusive, the Mona Lisa type. He forbade her to appear in public, in cafés, or on dance floors to preserve the illusion of her being a woman who suffered in silence. Clara was not pleased with the plan, saying: "Poop to the public! What's the good of making all this money if I can't have any fun?"[3]

In the meantime, the exuberant Selznick still had not built his future studio. Therefore, he had to rent an available one in Fort Lee: Alice Guy-Blaché's Solax studio. In his new position as director general of the Clara Kimball Young Film Corporation, Capellani was interviewed several times by the trade and general press. In these interviews, he revealed an ambivalent attitude toward the American production system. Capellani stated:

> You can't make photoplays as you make shoes. There are too many motion picture factories in America and too few real studios. Producing a motion picture is an art, not a job. You can't turn your studio into a machine shop, your actors into mill hands and your directors into foremen and expect to produce artistic and appealing creations that will elevate the screen above the sordid and commonplace and place the motion picture on the plane with its allied arts of drama, literature and music.
>
> The standardization of the feature picture into five reels is one of the greatest drawbacks of the advancement of our art. You might as well tell a novelist just how many words he must write his next story in, or a painter how many brushfuls of paint he must use on his next canvas. The majority of stories produced as five-reel pictures today could have been done infinitely better in three

reels. On the other hand many a wonderful story has been ruined by the necessity of cutting it to five reels.[4]

Even though the American film industry had enabled him to become a household name, Capellani was annoyed by the production system. He felt the director should have total control over the production. He was also opposed to some of the new developments in film technique:

> America has made tremendous strides artistically as commercially in the production of pictures. If there is any tendency more than another that I have noticed and would criticise it is the too free use of the "close-up" and the apparent timidity of directors as to the sustained length of a scene. The "close-up" is an extremely useful bit of photographic technique, but it must not be overdone. It should be used just as the spectator in a theater uses his opera glasses—for occasional magnified glimpses of the players, in order to register more powerfully certain moments in the progress of the story. No one wants to sit in the front row of a theater all the time nor watch half a play through opera glasses.
>
> The chopping up of big scenes into short lengths with little "flashbacks" to unimportant details and outside happenings is getting to be a nuisance. The biggest scene in the [Henry] Bernstein play "The Thief" was forty-five minutes long and between two people only.[5] There is no reason why a big scene in a picture cannot be sustained straight through to its climax without a single flashback or cut-in that isn't absolutely essential to the immediate action.[6]

That Capellani still thought of motion pictures in such theatrical terms is astonishing. For a modern audience, the use of the close-up is so obvious that it's hard to see why Capellani was so reluctant to use it. Nevertheless, we should not forget he had been in America only for a year, and prewar French pictures were almost completely devoid of close-ups. According to Capellani, in order to make a good picture, you needed a good story, and no technical tricks could remedy a bad one: "If I were asked for a percentage table on what makes a great picture I would say 50 per cent story, 30 per cent star, and 20 per cent director. Judging by the average picture we see today, the percentage table as compiled in the producing company's office would read: 50 per cent advertising, 40 per cent star, and 10 per cent direction, with no story at all."[7]

His attitude may have been rather cynical, but it was certainly close to the truth. He had to work with Lewis J. Selznick, a high-tempered character, and produce vehicles to make Clara Kimball Young shine as never before. While he accepted this assignment, he still wanted to do the best job he could. As Capellani was preparing Clara's next feature, *The Common Law* (1916), a journalist was sent to the studio to observe the master at work. There he noticed a huge sign above the sets ordering the actors to "BE NATURAL."[8] The resulting article provides a fine description of the director:

> One's first impression of Capellani is that of geniality. It shines from his big boyish eyes; it oozes from the finger-tips that clasp in a firm, hearty hand-shake; it even peeks out in the smile hidden behind those bushy wind-shields that decorate the lower-half of his head. And it isn't that surface sort of geniality, either. It lies far deeper than his true Parisian politeness and hearty laughter. Its proof is in the devotion of the men and women who have worked with him in almost all his American productions—and the adoration of his wife and children.[9]

Capellani calmly exercised his authority over a faithful group of technicians he gathered around him. He knew he would get better results with kindness and consideration. Unlike Josef von Sternberg, who later terrorized actors, Capellani liked to give them confidence in themselves.[10] Capellani thought, "Screen acting should be nature herself. What your Shakespeare—he calls the mirror up to nature. The camera—he does not lie. He tells the truth—always the truth. If you are beautiful—he says so, on the screen; if you are not—not! If you make a grimace, *voilà!* on the screen—the monkey-face. My artistes—they must be natural. That is why I am what you say—so gentle with them. If I give the big shout and call them by their bad names—what happens? *Pouf!* They get the nerves—they try. Oh! So hard they try to ACT—an' when they try it is worse. The more they try—the worser. *Tiens!* I speak soft, always soft. I try to show them what it is they must register. I coax—that is the word—I coax them, to be natural, to walk, and talk like the real people."[11]

The journalist observed Capellani giving instructions to his actors. He spoke so softly you could not hear him ten feet away. He took them to a small enclosure in which the action was to take place. He explained in his delightful English what he wanted. When he addressed his brother Paul, he did so in machine-gun French. A still photograph from this time shows Capellani in his shirtsleeves on a parallel, megaphone in hand, directing a scene with a large crowd of extras. Clara Kimball Young sits beside him on the platform, smiling, while Paul Capellani chats with actor Conway Tearle, who is examining the script.

Ben Carré did not follow Capellani to Selznick's new company. He remembered what happened: "He asked me to join them with the promise of a better salary. To tell the truth, I was committed voluntarily only to Tourneur and the larger salary was very tempting. I talked to Jules Brulatour who came almost every day to the studio and I insisted to tell him of the chance for me to make more money. Before I could finish he told me that this new company could not go on, to forget about it, and he increased my salary—which had remained the same since I came to America. As Capellani had such confidence in my work, I felt the necessity to help him by speaking to Henri Ménessier, my colleague from France, who had been responsible for me to join Gaumont in Paris. I knew he was going to quit Solax studio and return to France. The two talked together and I was relieved; I was still with Tourneur with fifteen dollars more each week, and Capellani and Ménessier were agreeable to each other."[12]

Henri Ménessier thus became Capellani's art director from that point on. For *The Common Law,* Capellani pioneered some innovative techniques in building the sets. An article of the time reported that he "constructed an entire nine-room apartment and had it furnished to the minutest detail. By rolling the camera a few feet at a time he can 'shoot' any part of the big setting."[13] Other fellow Frenchmen also worked with Capellani, in particular cameraman Jacques Montéran and assistant director Marcel Morhange.

Selznick spared no expense in advertising his first independent production. Practically every week articles appeared in trade papers about the progress of the production, giving the address of company headquarters as 49th Street and Seventh Avenue. On June 3, 1916, Capellani had already started to work on the script, which was adapted from Robert W. Chambers's novel. Clara Kimball Young was on holiday and was to be back on July 16 to start shooting. At the beginning of July, Capellani selected the supporting cast. The advertising campaign was ready with the publication of a special photoplay edition of the novel (with stills from the film), which would be available in newsstands across the country. On August 5, Conway Tearle was hired to play the male lead. He would soon become Mary Pickford's leading man in the superb *Stella Maris* (1918), directed by Marshall Neilan. Paul Capellani was also included in the cast as the villain. Albert's next production was mentioned on August 12—*The Foolish Virgin* (1916) with

Clara Kimball Young. By September 9, the shooting of *The Common Law* was over, and Selznick organized a screening of sequences of the film—which had not yet been edited—for a crowd of enthusiastic exhibitors. The producer was planning the film's release in the minutest detail. Nevertheless, the shooting proved far longer than usual, resulting in a film of seven, rather than the regular five, reels. Preview screenings were organized in New York and Chicago. As the film looked like a great success, the company decided to print 100 copies, the highest number ever printed for a picture in those days.

Reviews were good. One noted, "*The Common Law* . . . is truly a remarkable production. . . . Continuity throughout the picture could hardly be improved upon, and the story is smoothly narrated on the screen with the use of fewer subtitles than many productions of shorter length. The subtitles, too, are made artistically attractive by the use of decorative designs. Director-General Albert Capellani has lent artistic touches to the whole that add to the production's worth. Many of the settings, particularly in the studio scenes, are magnificent. . . . On the whole, *The Common Law*, will prove a box office magnet."[14] However, *Variety* was skeptical as to the box-office potential of the picture: "As a money-getter *The Common Law* will prove a box-office attraction of the first rank, but it is a picture that one will have to play more than a day in order to get the benefit of the cumulative advertising value."[15]

The film contains a sequence where the character played by Young becomes a model and has to disrobe for a painter, played by Conway Tearle. All the reviewers praised the director's handling of this scene, noting that he managed to suggest nudity while avoiding the vulgar. "The posing scenes Capellani has handled adorably. In making the disrobing girl sit in a heavy-armed Roman chair which reveals most disconcerting flashes while keeping modesty within perfect censorial bounds, he exhibited Gallic wit."[16]

The Common Law is still considered a lost film. We can

therefore rely only on reviewers' comments. They all appreciated the French touch brought by Capellani: "[His] excellence
lies more in his exquisite valuation of detail and finesse than in
breadth and power such as Griffith's and Brenon's. He is as
subtle as his mother-tongue; he gets his effects by a stealthy
artistry that sneaks up from behind one, as it were, and stabs
the heart via the back ribs."[17] Screenwriter Lenore Coffee, who
later worked with Clara Kimball Young, described in detail the
undressing sequence: "When [his model] appeared she was not
only young and beautiful, but obviously a lady. He tried to
make certain she understood what the pose was to be. She
nodded, and he motioned to a screen behind which she could
undress. Now this is where subtlety entered into sex scenes,
sometimes with more impact than total revelation. You saw her
hand just move one panel of the screen aside, then you saw
Conway facing the opening and staring, unable to believe his
eyes. After a long pause, he gave a shivery sigh and the title
read, 'I suppose you realize that you are practically flawless?' I
believe the audience saw that naked girl through Conway's
eyes just as if the girl herself had faced them."[18]

The story of *The Common Law* can be summed up as follows. Following the death of her mother, Valerie West (Clara
Kimball Young) is left destitute. She becomes the model of
two painters, and they both fall in love with her. The first one,
Querida (Paul Capellani), is a Spaniard and a womanizer who
refuses marriage. The other, Neville (Conway Tearle), comes
from a reputable family, which doesn't like Valerie. Besides, he
is already engaged to another girl. After numerous misunderstandings, Valerie ends up killing Querida, who tried to rape
her, and returns to Neville, who is ready to marry her. The
critics were unanimous in their praise of the lead actors, including Paul Capellani, who, as Querida, "does the best work he
has put upon American films."[19] Paul managed his career fault-
lessly, going from heartthrob to cad, a change in casting
unusual for the United States. He received a typed letter from

a fan who had been particularly impressed by his successive characterizations:

Lakewood, O. 12/6/16.

Mr. Paul Capellani,
c/o C Young Picture Studio,
New York City, N.Y.

Dear Sir:—

I take off my hat to you as the most excellent and versatile film performer in the world.

After having seen you a number of times, in your many splendid plays, most of them so true to life, I beg leave to thank you very much for the pleasure and entertainment given me and also wish you the success of many more years to come, and also hope to see you many more times.

Although I have never met you nor shakened [*sic*] your hand, I wish to ask you, if you should ever stop in Cleveland to make a visit to please advertise it a little before time, so that many of your Cleveland admirers may have the pleasure of seeing the man who has tried his best to please the criticising public and has so splendidly succeeded, may his fame be everlasting!

I should highly appreciate if you would send me your photo with your autograph upon it.

I think that I have taken up enough of your very valuable time and will close now with again wishing you the success of many more years to come, and hoping to hear from you in the near future and also thanking you in advance for any favours you may extend to me, I beg to remain,

Respectfully yours,

D. Ahlgrimm,
1274 Fry St Lakewood, O.[20]

This very respectful fan letter was not always the kind received by film stars of the time. Screenwriter Lenore Coffee was in charge of Clara Kimball Young's fan mail in 1919. Among the letters Young received were some obscene ones, which were sometimes sent to the police.

After *The Common Law,* which was adapted from a contemporary novel, Capellani turned to another novel for his next film, *The Foolish Virgin* (1916), adapting the book by Thomas Dixon, the controversial author of *The Clansman,* which D. W. Griffith had recently filmed as *The Birth of a Nation* (1915). In October 1916, Capellani began shooting his new film with the same leading players as in the previous production. The subject seemed very much in line with Griffith's high-blown melodramas. Mary (Clara Kimball Young) is a young, romantic schoolteacher who falls in love with Jim (Conway Tearle), thinking he is her knight in shining armor. Instead, she discovers he is a burglar. When her mother tries to kill him, Mary arranges his cure by a doctor (Paul Capellani). All's well that ends well: Jim follows the path of redemption.

The Foolish Virgin did not receive the enthusiastic reception of *The Common Law.* According to *Photoplay,* the picture "is little less than a disaster, considering the prominence of the star, the resources of the company, and the fine record of the director. How did Capellani happen to perpetrate so tiresome a thing?"[21] Other reviewers were less severe: "Characterized by splendid direction and acting is *The Foolish Virgin,* the Selznick picture featuring Clara Kimball Young. Albert Capellani had adapted and produced this story by Thomas Dixon in his own style—one is tempted to say in his inimitable style. Throughout the nearly seven reels one sees the hand of the master craftsman. Subtitles are scarce; for that matter no more than are shown are needed."[22] *Variety* ignored the film altogether, a bad sign.

Capellani made one last picture for Lewis J. Selznick. *The*

Easiest Way (1917) was adapted from a play by Eugene Walter, first produced in 1909. Laura Murdock (Clara Kimball Young) is a penniless young actress who agrees to be kept in style by a wealthy broker, Brockton (Joseph Kilgour). Shortly afterward, she falls in love with a young journalist, John Madison (Rockcliffe Fellowes). The young man decides to go away to try to make money enough to marry her. Left alone, unable to find work, Laura goes back to Brockton. When Madison returns, ready to marry her, he discovers her unfaithfulness. After the breakup, Laura tries to drown herself. She is rescued, however, and finds happiness in Madison's arms.

A remake of this Capellani film was produced at the beginning of the sound era under the same title, *The Easiest Way* (1931), directed by Jack Conway, with Constance Bennett, Adolphe Menjou, and Robert Montgomery. The storyline was updated; in the talkie version, Laura does not try to kill herself. Conway's version, like the best pre-Code pictures of that era, offers an interesting comment on the have-nots of American society who aspire to a better life. Capellani's original version also focuses on the social aspect, but in a different time. His Laura is a third-rate actress who travels with a group of chorus girls from town to town. One of the title cards gives a clue why Laura decided to have an easy life: "Why did you leave me alone? What chance has a woman to fall and rise again?" Capellani's film incurred the censors' wrath. In Pennsylvania, the State Board of Censors wanted to cut a whole reel from the seven-reel feature. The Selznick Corporation had to organize a special screening to be able to release the film untouched.

The Easiest Way was released in April 1917 to excellent reviews. "Nothing but praise was heard for the excellent direction of Albert Capellani and it was agreed that Miss Young has never done better screen work. This is particularly evident in the close-ups which are exceptionally numerous and exceptionally well done."[23] "When a photoplay can hold you for 7,400 feet after you are already familiar with the story, it is the best test of worth.[24] Miss Young has never done any finer film acting than in this picture. She is ideal for the star part."[25] "Only one thing could make such a story acceptable to people of intelligence and the right moral outlook—its truth. As a page from life, the life of temptation and bitter disillusion that many women are forced to lead in the struggle for a livelihood, *The Easiest Way* effects no compromise with facts. . . . Albert Capellani's direction is excellent throughout."[26]

Just why Capellani left Selznick's company is unknown. Perhaps he wanted to have more of a say in the choice of subjects. He certainly did not want to be in charge only of the company's star vehicles and be forced to go on making stereotyped melodramas. He accepted the star system and recognized it was an essential tool to bring in revenue. At the same time, as he was quoted as saying in one published report, he thought that "to begin with, pictures are generally rushed through because the stars are too highly paid that to take time to direct a film as it ought to be done means a waste of money. Too much is paid to those chosen few. The money ought to be more evenly distributed. A certain sum is, as a rule, set apart for each picture. So much for the star, so much for setting and other incidentals. The star gets the major portion, leaving next to nothing for the rest of the expenses. To me it is like buying a very beautiful diamond and then having it set in a cheap, tawdry setting."[27]

There was also the irritating Mr. Selznick. With his glibness and publicity stunts, Selznick had managed to get on the wrong side of the film industry. Capellani was a personality to be reckoned with and was not ready to accept compromises. As for Clara Kimball Young, she only wished to "smoke cigarettes, drink champagne, and spit in the public's eye."[28] She left Selznick before the end of her contract, after meeting Harry Garson, with whom she fell in love. Garson was going to manage her career, which would slowly decline during the 1920s. Lewis J. Selznick would end up bankrupt in 1923. This defeat would ironically push two of his sons to work in the film industry in order to restore his image and their family's reputation. Myron would become one of Hollywood's most prestigious agents, and his brother David—who added an O. as his middle initial—would become the most flamboyant independent producer of the Golden Age of Hollywood. They both remained extremely close to their father.

13

Transition at Mutual

In June 1917, Capellani signed a contract with John R. Freuler, the president of Mutual Film Corporation. Once again, he was hired to direct the new star of the studio, Julia Sanderson, then a Broadway actress. It seems he could not escape his image of being a woman's director. Capellani declared he was "more than delighted with the prospect of directing Miss Sanderson."[1] *Motion Picture News* announced that their first film together was on the way, and the notice advised exhibitors to book it.[2] In fact, Capellani never directed Julia Sanderson, and she only made one film, *The Runaway* (1917), directed by Dell Henderson.[3]

Capellani made only two pictures at Mutual. In September 1917, he was shooting *American Maid* with Edna Goodrich and William B. Davidson. The film was made at the Glendale Empire All Star Corporation studios in Long Island. The plot deals with a contemporary theme: a middle-class girl volunteers for the Red Cross and cures wounded soldiers back from the front. The picture's quality seemed a real decline compared with previous Capellani productions. It was only a five-reeler, and *Variety* was scathing about it: "An inane, badly directed, and generally butchered program feature. . . . *American Maid* seems to have been made some time ago, at least the greater portion. Then someone discovered how bad it was and a new introduction was written. This embodies the war atmosphere, and it is the best section, although all sorts of liberties have been taken, and it has been padded in places."[4] With such a review, we wonder how much of the film Capellani actually directed.

His other Mutual production received even less press when released in April 1918, six months after Capellani left Mutual. *The Richest Girl* (1918), with Ann Murdock and David Powell, was a comedy about a young heiress who hides her real identity to win the love of a penniless young man. The film was memorable for just one thing: it was Paul Capellani's last film under his brother's direction. His part was actually rather small; he was really a supporting player. At this point, Paul was looking for a career move. He wanted to become a director. For now, though, he continued acting, in particular for Ivan Abramson's *One Law for Both* (1917), which dealt with Russian immigrants in America and the different ways a fallen woman and a fallen man are treated within the community.

As for Albert, he certainly did not appreciate his time at Mutual. In some interviews he revealed that he disliked small-budget, rough-job productions. He left Mutual in October 1917 for a more affluent production company that he thought would offer better prospects. The trade press announced he had signed a contract with Richard A. Rowland, the president of Metro Pictures Corporation. "With great facilities for producing big features at his disposal, together with the most talented stars, Mr. Capellani feels that his affiliation with Metro Pictures Corporation will result in the making of the greatest pictures of his career."[5]

Paul's opportunity to become a director came from an Argentinean company, Platense-Film, which had capital of half a million dollars. The founders wanted to develop the company by hiring well-known professionals. Several French technicians were hired, including the cameraman Georges Benoit, who had worked with Raoul Walsh on *Regeneration* (1915), among other films; and Marcel Morhange, who had been Emile Chautard's and Albert Capellani's assistant. They signed a contract with Platense-Film in August 1917 at the same time as Paul Capellani.[6] The newly created film company was managed by Camilla Quiroga, an Argentinean film star, and her husband, Héctor. Paul directed a six-reeler in Buenos Aires called *¿Hasta Dónde . . . ?* (1918), where he shared the lead with Camilla Quiroga. Some of the local papers appreciated the picture, particularly Paul's acting in a dual role and Benoit's cinematography; but the trade press found the film mediocre. "We believe you cannot blame Mr. Capellani for this failure because his performance as an actor was not inferior to expectations, although as artistic director, due to difficulties of adapting to our environment which he was unaware of, some vivid sequences in the Paris of old were only just acceptable."[7] Basically, the production was described as costing a great deal of money and effort, leading to not very much.

It was not surprising, then, that by May 5, 1918, Paul was back in New York. Instead of returning to acting, however, Paul joined the French pictorial service in New York to produce a series of war propaganda documentaries in October 1918. The war was nearly over. *The Battle of Château-Thierry*—written and compiled by Paul Capellani—came out in December 1918 and was described as "a living memorial to American valour. The eye-witness to the indomitable courage of those to whom victory is due: The American and Allied soldiers."[8]

It may seem odd that Paul elected to direct this documentary: until then he had shown little interest in the war. But his own position was precarious. He had been discharged in July 1915 and probably had never been to the front line. If he ever wanted to return to France, he was going to need a "war record" of some kind, as public opinion in France was red-hot regarding patriotic duty. And there was the example of Maurice Tourneur. Having arrived in New York on May 1, 1914, he had been called back to France by general mobilization on August 3, 1914. He ignored the call and was declared a draft dodger in November 1914. His situation was regularized with the French authorities only in January 1921, when he became an American citizen. When the French press realized that he had been a deserter in wartime, he was violently attacked:

"Maurice Tourneur, we just learned, had, when the war was declared, a conduct towards his country amounting to desertion, as in 1915 [*sic*], he got himself naturalized as a citizen of the United States, where he had been living for two years. This desertion we condemn, as any Frenchman proud of his name should do."[9] When Tourneur returned to France for good in 1926, he would face a violent press campaign about his attitude during the war as well as numerous problems with French authorities.[10]

Paul and Albert never worked together in motion pictures after 1917. Paul returned to France at the beginning of 1919. He immediately got in touch with old acquaintances, in particular his mentor, André Antoine. "I would be very happy to see you and to talk with you for a few minutes," Paul wrote Antoine. "During the war, there has been some unfavorable talk about me, and often it was nonsense. It's time to clarify matters. I want to do it with you and with a few friends whose affection is precious to me."[11] Paul went back to work in Parisian theaters and studios. His American period was over.

Meanwhile, Albert was starting a new adventure at Metro Pictures Corporation.

14

Metro Director

Albert Capellani took a two-week holiday in Atlantic City before starting at Metro. He hated the heat and preferred the cool breeze of the Atlantic coast. In the middle of November 1917, he was already at work on *Daybreak* (1918), adapted from a Jane Murfin and Jane Cowl play. Capellani worked on the adaptation himself with June Mathis, who had a prominent position at Metro. As well as being a screenwriter, she held the position of artistic supervisor, meaning she had the duties of an executive producer. During the silent era, there were numerous women screenwriters; Bess Meredyth, Frances Marion, Anita Loos, Jeanie Macpherson, Lenore Coffee, and Jane Murfin were the most famous. This predominantly female profession during the early days of motion pictures would become mainly masculine when the power of the studio became dominant. Also, with the advent of talking pictures, many women screenwriters would lose their jobs in favor of cheaper male screenwriters from Broadway.

Inside the Metro studios, Capellani's new project was begun under excellent conditions. He was given a cast of professional stage actors. In the leads were Emily Stevens and the British actor Julian L'Estrange as well as a young beginner called Evelyn Brent, who would become the star of several of Josef von Sternberg masterpieces a decade later. The plot of *Daybreak* concerns Arthur Frome (Julian L'Estrange), an alcoholic businessman, and his wife, Edith (Emily Stevens), who decides to leave him. When she returns to her husband a few years later, she gives no explanation about her conduct. He suspects she has been unfaithful and discovers she had a child.

Actually, he is the father; Edith preferred to leave him rather than raise a child with an alcoholic father. After Arthur survives an attempt on his life by a jealous husband, the couple is happily reunited. With such a melodramatic plot, Capellani's picture received faint praise: "The feature is very well handled in production. The studio sets showing the home of the Fromes are wonderfully well done, so well they were mistaken by a great many for the genuine. There are no exteriors to speak of except brief street scenes. The photography has evidently been pulled through by very clever tinting and lighting. The light effects are corking at times, but the like cannot be said for the general camera work. David Calcagni did the shooting for this picture."[1]

In February 1918, Capellani collaborated with June Mathis on an adaptation of the famous Edith Wharton novel *The House of Mirth*. In fact, many new projects were crowding in on him at this time: he was also preparing a picture for May Allison entitled *Social Hypocrites* (1918) as well as a production with the Broadway star Alla Nazimova. May Allison's movie was put into production first. The film takes place in the 1870s, allowing the Metro costume department to create dresses with full skirts and long trains. Hairdos were similarly of the period, with high pompadours and long curls. As before, the picture was almost entirely shot in the studio. Capellani had an excellent cast of leading and supporting players to work with. The story is set among the British aristocracy. Young Leonore (May Allison) is rejected from polite society because her father, Colonel Fielding (Frank Currier), died penniless, disowned by his family. She is a victim of the scheming Lady Vanessa Norton (Stella Hammerstein), who accuses Leonore of cheating at a bridge game. Eventually Leonore finds love by marrying Frank Simpson (Henry Kolker). Once again, Capellani's picture was praised for the quality of its sets. *Variety* noted, "The story is well connected and holds interest throughout. As a programme feature, it's as good as the majority and better than many."[2]

After these two average Metro pictures, *The House of Mirth* (1918) would be of an altogether different caliber. The film-makers first thought of Emmy Wehlen to play Lily Bart, but in the end, Katherine Harris Barrymore was hired to play the young victim of New York high society's hypocrisy.[3] Edith Wharton's gloom-and-doom novel describes a society that judges only by appearances. Lily Bart is raised by a rich aunt, but is left penniless after her death. Having rejected a rich suitor, she is forced to seek employment. Lily becomes the victim of a married couple, who use her as a decoy to hide their adultery. Humiliated, she tries to commit suicide, but is saved at the last minute by lawyer Lawrence Selden (Henry Kolker). Unlike the movie, the novel ends with Lily's death—Capellani probably had to provide a happy ending to satisfy the producers.

In spite of these concessions, some reviewers were put off by the relentlessly dark story. The reviewer for *Variety* wrote: "It has been scenarioized [*sic*] by June Mathis for Metro, directed by Albert Capellani, photographed by Eugene Gaudio, all of it with rare excellence for the respective efforts, but the layout is not a good one for a feature picture for the reason that the majority of the principals are a rotten set, not worth wasting time over, especially as none of them get their just desserts. They are permitted to continue their various immoral paths. Such a series of despicable types for principals has seldom been gathered into one set of principals—and they are all the more so through being played by stellar artists. . . . A distinctly rotten mess, well produced."[4] Others were less severe: "Without unduly accentuating unpleasant situations the director has succeeded well in turning the finer points of the story to account, and Katherine Harris Barrymore has given a splendid portrayal of a character which, regardless of its human tendency to err, upholds the dignity of moral womanhood."[5] "Director Capellani is certainly deserving of much credit for the intelligent way he has handled this offering. Despite the unusual number of complications and the large cast involved, he has made the production understandable and interesting all the way, at the same time maintaining the suspense and giving us many good individual touches throughout."[6]

Capellani followed up these features with a prestige production involving a newly recruited Metro star, the Russian stage actress Alla Nazimova. Born Adelaida Leventon in Yalta, Nazimova was trained by Constantin Stanislavski in Moscow's Art Theatre. Only after she immigrated to the United States in 1905 did she become a star, playing the heroines in works by Henrik Ibsen and Anton Chekhov in New York. Her first film—*War Brides* (1916), under the direction of Herbert Brenon—was made for Lewis J. Selznick. But it proved to be a false start; she went back to the stage, where she played a dual role in *'Ception Shoals,* a play by H. Austin Adams. Maxwell Karger, who was in charge of production at Metro, saw her in the play and decided to hire her for the firm. He was sure that Nazimova had enormous potential for the screen. She first made two lurid sexual melodramas for Metro, *Revelation* (1918) and *Toys of Fate* (1918), both directed by George D. Baker. Nazimova's contract gave her the right to select her own stories, and she asked the studio to acquire the rights of a play by Belgian playwright Henry Kistemaeckers, *L'Occident.* June Mathis, in charge of script and production, selected Albert Capellani to direct Nazimova. Mathis felt that Nazimova needed a director who understood actresses. And she felt that Capellani had done a great job directing Clara Kimball Young. He would also bring more prestige to the production.

In June 1918, Metro officially acquired the rights of *L'Occident. Moving Picture World* announced that "Albert Capellani will direct Mme. Nazimova, and much is expected from this brilliant combination of star and director. Mr. Capellani has long been an admirer of the great Russian's dramatic gifts, and Mme. Nazimova is delighted that the celebrated Frenchman is to be her director. In collaboration with

June Mathis, Mr. Capellani is now engaged in making a scenario of the drama."[7] Capellani hired actor Henry Kolker to be his assistant director and also to help him select the cast.

The play's original title, *L'Occident*, was changed to *Eye for Eye* (1918), a title chosen by Nazimova herself.[8] She plays Hassouna, the daughter of a sheik who falls in love with a captain of the Foreign Legion (Charles Bryant).[9] She helps the officer escape from prison, and in retaliation is sold at a slave market. Hassouna becomes a circus dancer and again meets her beloved captain, who adopts her. Alas, her love turns to hatred when she learns he killed members of her tribe, including her loved ones. She seeks revenge by seducing the captain's nephew. The captain, however, is not guilty of this offense, and eventually the two are reunited. The lurid melodramatic plot sounds silly, but it is typical of the kind of stories Nazimova was looking for. Moreover, movie audiences loved this kind of escapism.

As with previous Metro films, the production values were praised, in particular the sets, costumes, supporting cast, and general atmosphere of the feature. *Variety* noted: "*Eye for Eye* is a Metro picture in which Nazimova has a part that suits her admirably, and which few others could have played. . . . The picture is elaborately and painstakingly produced, the atmosphere of the desert being indicated remarkably well, and with great artistry. The picture, which is in seven reels, is much too long as the slender plot does not justify it. Nazimova, as the fugitive, sinuous Bedouin plays splendidly, and completely looks the character. . . . The photography is sharp and clear, and of great beauty."[10] The feature received praise from the trade press; one reviewer noted: "This much talked of Nazimova film looks to me like a certain winner. It has quality all through for Director Albert Capellani has gone to the limit in supplying a richly artistic production in which the famous Russian actress registers a characterization that could not be touched by our less temperamental American players. . . . Get this by all means and don't worry if you go a trifle above your customary price for the picture will justify the expenditure if you handle it properly."[11]

Even before editing was complete on *Eye for Eye,* Capellani started shooting Nazimova's next feature, adapted from *'Ception Shoals.* In October 1918, during the day he was shooting *Out of the Fog* (the title selected for the *'Ception Shoals* adaptation) and during early mornings and lunchtimes he was editing *Eye for Eye.* And, last but not least, in the evenings he was writing the script of *The Red Lantern,* his third Nazimova vehicle. He even found time to direct a propaganda short entitled *A Woman of France* (1918), in which Nazimova promoted the sale of Liberty Bonds. Capellani must have been exhausted with such a heavy schedule. Certainly, his diabetes was beginning to be a serious handicap. Untreated diabetes leads to severe complications: high blood pressure, kidney failure, retinopathy, heart failure, and foot ulcers. Capellani never seemed to follow a strict diet. He loved his food, didn't stint himself, and remained stout until the end. For the moment, however, he managed to keep up with the pace of American production.

Out of the Fog was released in February 1919. The film gave Nazimova the opportunity to avoid her usual exotic vamp part. She played a dual role, mother and daughter. Although the film was a runaway melodrama, it seems to have been an impressive production. Henri Ménessier, who was its art director, remembered, "I can say without being unduly excessive that it was the best picture Capellani ever made."[12] The picture was shot on location in Gloucester, Massachusetts, along the Atlantic coast, by a lighthouse. Following the death of her fiancé, Faith (Nazimova) gives birth to a daughter. Her brother Job (Henry Harman), a religious fanatic, pushes her to commit suicide. She drowns herself in the ocean. Twenty years later, Faith's daughter, Eve (Nazimova), who has been raised by her uncle, has been kept away from any human contact. She meets the captain of a yacht, Philip Blake (Charles Bryant), who needs her to help one of his passengers give birth to a baby. After Philip and his ship have left, Job intercepts a letter the captain has written to Eve. When Philip returns, Job tells him that Eve is dead. The girl is in fact locked inside the lighthouse, and in the end Philip manages to rescue her.

Critics praised Nazimova's performance. An analysis of the picture's box-office potential reached this conclusion: "In some roles there is no finer screen actress than Nazimova, and with each picture her hold is becoming stronger with regular fans, also with theatergoers who are interested in truly artistic impersonations. The picture is so far out of the ordinary in its possession of artistic qualities that I would make a special appeal to the most critical element in your community."[13] *Variety* noted, "*Out of the Fog* has an idea to convey and does so in a most convincing manner through the medium of Nazimova and Henry Harman. The picture at all times holds and in its tenser situations could not be improved upon. Lucid, in perfect continuity, a fine story and good situations, it will please those who look for bigger things in the silent drama. . . . *Out of the Fog* is a high standard picture, fine in technique and well lighted."[14]

Out of the Fog received special praise from the National Board of Review for its artistry. The organization arranged for a special screening of the Capellani picture together with Victor Sjöström's *Tösen från Stormyrtorpet* (*The Girl from the Marsh Croft*, 1917), both considered high artistic achievements in terms of cinematography and acting[15]—which makes the loss of this Capellani feature all the more tragic. The use of location shooting, particularly spectacular seascapes, explained the board's pairing *Out of the Fog* with one of the best Swedish silent films of the era, a time when the Swedes were incomparable in their dramatic use of natural landscape.

At the end of October 1918, Albert Capellani left for Hollywood with his wife and children. Metro had decided to move its production headquarters to California and to close for good its East Coast studios. The decision was not only the result of the steady increase in film production on the West Coast, but also because of the Spanish flu pandemic, which was affecting the whole world at the time. It was thought that film crews would be safer in the warm California climate during wintertime. This pandemic killed more people than the Great War itself had; it is estimated that at least thirty million people died from this particularly virulent strain of the virus. The film industry was affected like every part of the population. One of the most tragic losses was the death of the young and talented filmmaker John H. Collins at the age of twenty-eight. Married to actress Viola Dana, who often played the lead in his pictures, he had an attractive personality and demonstrated real dramatic sense in *Children of Eve* (1915) and *Flower of the Dusk* (1918).[16] The young director was getting ready to follow the Metro production exodus to California when he died in October 1918.

15

The Red Lantern

Crossing the continent for the first time since his arrival in the United States, Capellani traveled to California at the end of October 1918. We can imagine it was a long and epic journey similar to King Vidor's from his native Texas to California in a Model T Ford. The more affluent Capellani traveled in his sumptuous Packard, but he found the heat unbearable in Texas and Arizona. He sold the car once he arrived in Hollywood.

The whole of the Metro technical staff moved west as well: screenwriter June Mathis, art director Henri Ménessier, technical director E. J. Shulter, and cameraman Eugene Gaudio. They were preparing the most ambitious Nazimova production of all.

The Red Lantern was adapted from an Edith Wherry novel set in the China of the Boxer Rebellion of 1899–1901. The author was the daughter of a Presbyterian missionary and had lived in China until the age of fifteen. However, the image of China and its inhabitants as depicted in *The Red Lantern* corresponded to the usual racial prejudices of the time. People were scared by the "Yellow Peril," and Chinese people were often portrayed as evil characters who practiced mutilations and lived according to ancient customs. The contemporary press nevertheless praised the quality of the re-creation, which was probably in accordance with the views of the average spectator. As usual, the lead characters were played by European actors wearing makeup. Alla Nazimova played Mahlee, a Eurasian born of a Chinese girl and a British aristocrat. Noah Beery, Wallace Beery's elder brother, played the stereotyped dyed-in-the-wool Oriental villain, of the kind often seen in

1920s and 1930s melodramas. He was Wang, a Eurasian who wanted to avenge himself on the Europeans, who had given him an education but rejected him socially.

For the script, Albert Capellani again collaborated with June Mathis. In their story, Mahlee (Nazimova) is raised by her grandmother, Mrs. Ling (Margaret McWade), and kept ignorant of her origins. When Mrs. Ling is at death's door, however, she reveals to Mahlee that she is a half-breed and tells her she needs to amputate her long feet, which are unbound, or she will be excluded from Chinese society. Mahlee can't do it. Saved by the Templetons, who are English missionaries, she converts to Christianity and becomes a schoolteacher in their mission. She falls in love with Andrew (Darrell Foss), the son of the Templetons. The young man ignores Mahlee after the arrival of the beautiful Blanche Sackville (played also by Nazimova), who happens to be Mahlee's half-sister. Meanwhile, Mahlee is subjected to the unwanted advances of Sam Wang (Noah Beery), a Eurasian who studied medicine in America, but nevertheless seeks revenge on the Westerners who despise him. Realizing she'll never be able to marry Andrew, Mahlee becomes Wang's ally in his crusade against foreigners. Wang is one of the leaders of the Boxer Rebellion. Mahlee dresses up as the Goddess of the Red Lantern to urge the people to rise up against foreigners. But once she hears that the mission is to be attacked, she runs to warn her father, Sir Philip Sackville (Frank Currier). She finally commits suicide by taking poison, as she cannot be accepted in any community.

The Red Lantern is available as a DVD, transferred from a print running 1,731 meters (5,679 feet) out of the original 2,000 meters (6,561 feet).[1] Unlike the other Nazimova Metro productions, which are lost, we can still see and enjoy this sumptuous film. It was the most prestigious and the most profitable of Nazimova's pictures at Metro. The production was huge, with no fewer than 800 Chinese extras used for some sequences. The filmmakers hired James Wang to select extras from Los Angeles's Chinatown.[2] He was also used to translate the director's instructions to the extras. An anecdote reveals Capellani's resourcefulness. During the filming, he tried to get a smile from a Chinese extra with no success; the man remained expressionless. In desperation, Capellani asked the actor if he would like some fungus soup. Immediately, the man grinned happily.[3] Very few Chinese-Americans made a career in the film industry. Anna May Wong was one of the rare exceptions. The young actress, then only fourteen, managed to get a part as an extra in one of the scenes in Capellani's movie.

According to Capellani, he shot the film in forty-one days, in January and February 1919.[4] Novelist Edith Wherry visited the set toward the end of January. Henri Ménessier's sets re-created a sumptuous Peking with its temples, open markets, missions, and crowded streets. He reproduced Peking's famous "Dragon Room," where the emperor's throne stood. Having spent so much time researching the subject together with Capellani and Mathis, Ménessier made watercolor sketches of all the interiors, which were later built. He also created a garden for the mission; and, for a colossal statue of the Goddess of Peace, sculptor Victor Andre copied a figure from a rare Chinese antique obtained by Capellani. The final statue was twenty-two feet tall and measured six feet across.[5] Again, Capellani's work encompassed not only the shooting itself but also the script and the art direction.

To direct the vast crowd of extras, Capellani divided them into groups. Each group was directed by an extra selected for that purpose. The crowd movements were rehearsed as many as five or six times, to make sure that everybody understood the instructions.[6] Some scenes were filmed at night, particularly the one where Mahlee appears as the Goddess of the Red Lantern, dressed in a magnificent costume adorned with thousands of pearls. The filmmakers used no fewer than six cameramen and 575 Chinese lanterns for this sequence.[7] To inspire the actors, a Chinese orchestra played during the filming.[8]

Metro organized a massive publicity campaign to launch the picture. The trade press mentioned a total cost of $250,000.[9] According to Capellani, however, the cost was closer to $90,000 (this probably excluded the star's salary), with box office receipts over a million dollars.[10]

The film was released in May 1919 and received raves from the press. *Variety* gushed: "With the release of *The Red Lantern*, Metro comes to fore and takes rank with the premiere producers of 'big' feature pictures. The veriest tyro can make no mistake about this. The combination of Nazimova and *The Red Lantern* is one of the most stupendous features ever undertaken in the limited history of filmdom. The enterprise is an undoubted success. . . . *The Red Lantern* is far and away the biggest thing Nazimova has ever done in pictures and many times the finest Metro has ever turned out."[11] Another review stated that the picture "stands not only as the most satisfactory production Nazimova has yet given us, but it ranks with the really big stories of the screen catalogue. . . . As a spectacle the production is a revelation. The scenes of the Feast of the Red Lantern are wonderfully well handled, both as to lighting effects and the direction of the mobs, while the scenes of the street fighting are well carried out."[12] Capellani's name was hardly ever mentioned in the reviews. This was foremost a Nazimova picture and a Richard Rowland and Maxwell Karger production—they were the heads of Metro.

Seen today, the picture retains its appeal, with its powerful crowd scenes and impressive production values. Nazimova is of course the main attraction. She manages to convey the character's tragic destiny. As a Eurasian, she is accepted neither by the Chinese nor by the Europeans. Because her feet were never bound, she is not considered Chinese. As for the Europeans, her skin color excludes her from society. The picture reflects the famous Rudyard Kipling saying from *The Ballad of East and West:* "East is East and West is West and never the twain shall meet." Among the racial prejudices of the time, miscegenation was one of the worst taboos. A contemporary reviewer suggested that a happy ending could have been filmed instead of a tragic one if only Mahlee were in reality a white woman, without a drop of Oriental blood. Had that been the case, she would have been allowed to marry her beloved and live happily ever after. This remark shows the extent of racial prejudice at the time. Interesting to note, however, is that in October 1919 D. W. Griffith released *Broken Blossoms,* in which he depicted Chinese immigrants in London's East End. In that film, Richard Barthelmess plays a young Chinese man in the slums of Limehouse who had come to Europe to bring the message of Buddha. This portrayal was certainly unusual in its sympathy with the Chinese character as hero at a time when most Chinese were shown as villains.

After a first release in May 1919, the picture was rereleased a month later following unprecedented box-office receipts. Richard Rowland spoke of the studio's strategy in the trade press. He rejected the idea of starring vehicles, which required highly expensive stars, he said. Nevertheless, he recognized that *The Red Lantern* with Nazimova was an exception to the rule, as it was so profitable. He went on to say, however, that he would like to promote big-budget pictures with lesser-known and less expensive actors. He captured perfectly the spirit of the times. In 1919, the film industry was feeling the effects of the postwar economic crisis, which brought a recession and a slump in production.

After the enormous success of *The Red Lantern,* Capellani had reached the heights of popularity and fame. However, he was far from happy with his own position at Metro. First of all, his salary was still just $500 a week, the same amount he was receiving at the World Film Corporation in 1916. The comparison with Nazimova's salary is telling. She was the highest-paid film star in the world, receiving $13,000 a week, a salary even greater than Mary Pickford's and Charlie Chaplin's. We know little of the Nazimova-Capellani relationship on the set.

But Nazimova was not the kind of star who took orders from anybody. On the stage, she liked to direct herself, and sometimes even her colleagues, even when she wasn't nominally the director. No doubt a conflict of egos developed. A few days after the shooting ended, Nazimova wrote a letter to her sister, Nina Leventon, highlighting the conflict:

> Capellani is no more. The thing that I could not bear any longer was seeing, and having to work with, a man who—no matter what one did—was constantly wearing an unhappy and unsatisfied face. Everything was not to his liking—the country, the people, the firm—until one day I asked him: "Is there anything that would ever make you happy?" And he said, "Yes—to be my own boss!" On account of my pictures being such a success he maintains that it is due to him and therefore he ought to be treated like Griffith. He constantly speaks of the adoration the latter is given in his studio, called "Master" instead of Mr. Griffith, etc. Also he wanted an increase of salary (750 a week instead of 500) and many other things that were impossible.[13]

Besides Capellani's conflict with Nazimova, the studio seems to have been unhappy with the cost of the production. Capellani shot more than 100,000 feet of film stock for *The Red Lantern* and therefore was "dipping too deeply into the company's coffers to make a financial hit with the stockholders."[14] If Metro complained, it was probably the last straw for Capellani. He decided to leave the company for good. As he told Nazimova, he wanted to become his own boss and to create his own company, like his former colleague Maurice Tourneur had done the previous year, and therefore achieve complete artistic control of his pictures.

As for Nazimova, her starring career was over five years later. She never worked again with a great director, favoring untalented men like Charles Bryant, whom she paraded as her husband. This allowed her to control her film image completely. This led to a slowly dwindling film career. In 1925, financially drained, she had to go back on the stage. For Nazimova as well, *The Red Lantern* would be the peak of her career.

16

Albert Capellani Productions, Inc.

To create a new independent film producing company in 1919 was a risky business. The postwar recession was starting to hit the motion-picture industry. Furthermore, small companies were quickly disappearing or being taken over by large corporations. In the mid-1920s, the great major film studios were formed; the few remaining independents would not be able to compete. Producer-directors, even the greatest, like D. W. Griffith, were going to have to bow to the major studios' power.

Capellani dreamed of having complete artistic control of his own films. He wanted to create pictures without interference from star or producer. He was willing to accept the risks. After all, he had the perfect profile for such a job, having been both an accountant and an administrator. He therefore believed he could cope in the jungle of the film industry. He was also influenced by his French colleagues, in particular Léonce Perret, who came to America in January 1917, as well as Maurice Tourneur, who arrived just before the war. Both of them had already created their own companies: in June 1918, Léonce created Perret Productions; and, in April of the same year, Maurice Tourneur Productions was incorporated.

On February 18, 1919, Capellani announced that he was about to create his own producing company.[1] It confirmed that his break from Metro had occurred immediately after the shooting of *The Red Lantern*. Capellani decided to leave California for good in February 1919. He never liked the place in any case and returned to Fort Lee, a town closer to a European lifestyle and with a cooler climate. He rented the Solax studios created by Alice Guy-Blaché, which were empty at the time. He had them refurbished and renamed Capellani studios; French producer Adolphe Osso became Capellani's general manager.[2] Henri Ménessier remained with Capellani as the new studio's art director. A couple of young actors, June Caprice and Creighton Hale, were hired to play leads. Comedienne Flora Finch, John Bunny's former partner at Vitagraph, was hired on March 11, 1919. The next day, the trade press announced that Capellani had signed a distribution agreement with Pathé-Exchange, the American branch of Pathé, to distribute his first feature produced under the Albert Capellani Productions banner. This would be *Oh, Boy!* (1919), which was adapted from the 1917 musical by Guy Bolton and P. G. Wodehouse, with a score written by Jerome Kern, who would later write *Show Boat*. Things were going so well, Capellani did not stop at this; on March 27 he signed Dolores Cassinelli, who had been the star of several of Léonce Perret's American productions. He also increased his stable of directors by hiring a young French filmmaker, George Archainbaud, on April 24. He also managed to regain the services of the masterful Lucien Andriot, who had worked with Capellani at the World Film Corporation, on May 5.[3] Within a few months, the company was up and running with actors, technical staff, a distributor, and several productions in preparation.

Oh, Boy! was completed by the end of April 1919 and was released in June, branded a "filmusical comedy," a neologism— or a publicity stunt—created especially for the film. In the leads, Capellani cast June Caprice, an ingénue who had worked for Fox, and Creighton Hale, who came from Pathé. The couple would appear together again on later Capellani productions. Albert Capellani gave himself a small part at the beginning of the picture, just as Alfred Hitchcock would do in his own films a few decades later. Albert had already given himself a cameo while at Pathé in *Le Nabab* (1913), where he appeared for a few moments as the captain of a ship. In *Oh, Boy!* he played the conductor in an orchestra pit as the curtain is about to rise, a fitting image for a filmmaker about to direct his actors. The story, created by Guy Bolton and his partner, the brilliant British humorist Pelham Grenville Wodehouse—the creator of the proverbial Jeeves—was in perfect tune with the times. College boy George Budd (Creighton Hale) wants to marry his girlfriend, Lou Ellen Carter (June Caprice). Alas, Lou Ellen's father refuses his consent because George likes to drink occasionally, and Judge Carter happens to be a fervent prohibitionist. Nevertheless, all will end well for the lovebirds when their parents, all of whom profess to be in favor of prohibition, are caught in a state of intoxication. The movie was released only a few months before the beginning of prohibition in the United States, which became the law in January 1920. The audience was well aware of this. In spite of the film's topicality, however, the reviews were disappointing. *Variety* noted: "*Oh, Boy!* is too long, but it will do. This production by Albert Capellani . . . was given a trade showing by Pathé this week, and overshot the endurance mark by at least a thousand feet, some 500 of which were given to work out an ending. . . . It is all light farce, never a serious moment, and it doesn't quite convince at any point during the six reels shown on the screen. In the whole course of this showing, which is admirably photographed—both interiors and exteriors are good—the director, judging by his work, seems like a man lost behind the scenes of a girl show. . . . The story itself is clean and will offend no one, except probably the prohibitionists."[4] The film met a similar reception in another trade paper: "Everybody worked hard to make this funny, but somehow the laughs aren't there. . . . Six reels is too much for a plot of this description. It is one thing to build up a musical comedy on a framework such as provided by P. G. Wodehouse and Guy Bolton, and quite another to make it answer the purpose of a prolonged feature film. Padding becomes necessary. In filling out this production undue prominence was accorded characters and scenes of relatively small importance."[5]

George Archainbaud directed two comedies for Capellani, both with Creighton Hale and June Caprice: *The Love Cheat* (1919), released in August; and *A Damsel in Distress* (1919), released in October. About *The Love Cheat,* an adaptation of a Tristan Bernard play entitled *Le Danseur inconnu* (*The Unknown Dancer*), *Variety* wrote: "Clear, accurate photography characterizes the production. There are some excellent long shots and a number of picturesque outdoor scenes shown around the home of the heroine. A generous number of close-ups are in evidence, probably due to the fact that the slight story needed assistance from some direction and appealed to the cameraman's art."[6] *A Damsel in Distress,* again adapted from P. G. Wodehouse, received better reviews: "The production is a delightful one from every angle, and George Archainbaud, who directed the production, has handled the story delightfully. The interior sets are perfect, and the lightings are all that could be asked."[7]

The company had thus managed to produce three features in a space of three months, a real achievement. Capellani then shot *The Virtuous Model* (1919) with Dolores Cassinelli, an adaptation of a French play by Pierre Wolf entitled *Le Ruisseau* (*The Gutter*). Henri Ménessier re-created Montmartre in great detail, with the Sacré-Cœur basilica and the silhouette of the Eiffel tower in the distance. It seemed that Capellani couldn't resist the idea of returning to his hometown on the screen. The story was typical melodrama, and was also later adapted for the screen in France by René Hervil as *Le Ruisseau* (1928). *The Virtuous Model* follows the destiny of Denise (Dolores Cassinelli), a poor girl living in the slums of Montmartre with her mother and making artificial flowers to make ends meet. Having lost her job, she ends up working in a cabaret, where she meets Paul Brehant (Vincent Serrano), a sculptor who asks her to pose nude for a statue. Denise refuses to disrobe; and Paul, impressed by her virtue, decides to marry her. After various misunderstandings with Paul's former mistress, Paul and Denise are reconciled for good. The plot resembled Capellani's earlier film *The Common Law* (1916) in some respects, in particular a titillating disrobing scene. *Variety* stated, "All this is sugar-coated melodrama, but it will go over. It is the stuff, despite its unreality, that gets the public."[8] *Moving Picture World* noted: "The production was made by Albert Capellani and is notable for the excellence of its character types and artistic handling. It is also unusually good in the matter of continuity and atmosphere. . . . It has here been elaborated with a great deal of voluptuous detail of an alluring type. There are moments when the treatment verges upon a sensuous extreme, such as the love scenes in the cabaret and the disrobing scene in the studio, but it is all done with sufficient delicacy to avoid actual offense. It is a production, however, which will undoubtedly make its greatest appeal with audiences of a highly sophisticated type."[9]

Albert and his family had not been back to France since their arrival in America. Now that the war was over, they could cross the Atlantic again without worrying about U-boats. And so, in July 1919, Capellani, his wife, and his children sailed for France for what would undoubtedly be a moving reunion. Once in Paris, Albert was interviewed by a journalist from *Le Film* and was asked to give his impressions of the state of the French film industry as an émigré filmmaker. His words on the state of his native country's industry sounded alarming. Capellani said, "I am a bit like a relation who left his family a long time ago, and who after several years comes back. He finds the old armchairs missing a leg, the kitchen in disrepair and there is no bathroom. . . . He is happy to be here, but he would like to find everything repaired and in good order. The studios have stayed a bit as they were. . . . Put back the legs missing on the armchairs, bring the studio up to date. We

Frenchmen showed in other industries—in nearly all of them—what we could do. Why shouldn't we recapture the place of honor for the film industry which we invented?"[10]

This disillusioned observation showed that he was not thinking of coming back to France for good. His situation in the United States was enviable compared with what had become of the once thriving French studios. During his stay, Capellani searched for new subjects. He bought the rights to various French plays. By October 9, 1919, he was back in New York. His family stayed in France a little longer and returned on November 22.

George Archainbaud, who during Capellani's absence had worked for the American Cinema company, came back to Capellani on October 6. A fourth and last June Caprice feature was put into production. This film, *In Walked Mary,* was again directed by Archainbaud, but not released until March 1920. Meanwhile, another director, Edwin Carewe, was also working with Dolores Cassinelli, under Capellani's supervision. His movie, *The Right to Lie* (1919), was inspired by a notorious criminal case, the prosecution of Harry K. Thaw in 1906 for the murder of architect Stanford White, who was alleged to have sexually abused Thaw's wife, Evelyn Nesbit. This scandalous case attracted the interest of film producers almost immediately, and several films based on the story were produced, such as *The Unwritten Law* (1907), produced by the Lubin Manufacturing Company. Capellani was therefore not the first to dramatize the real-life scandal. Years later, in 1955, Richard Fleischer would direct another feature film based upon that same affair, *The Girl on the Red Velvet Swing,* with Evelyn Nesbit herself as technical adviser. Nesbit had also starred in various dramas inspired by her life. Trade-paper notices regarding *The Right to Lie* suggested that it was a film for adults only: "This one will probably go big in a downtown house where you have a transient audience. If you have a select neighborhood house catering to the family trade it would be wise to look it over first as it is not the kind of a picture for innocent young girls to get excited over."[11]

Meanwhile, Capellani had already started his next feature, *The Fortune Teller* (1920) with Marjorie Rambeau, when an accident occurred that would severely handicap his company. On Saturday, December 20, 1919, a fire broke out in the Solax studio laboratories. It created an estimated $150,000 worth of damages, according to one source.[12] The *New York Times* cited damages amounting to $75,000 and stated that Capellani had lacerated a hand when he broke through a window to rescue the negative of *The Fortune Teller*.[13] The flames miraculously spared the studio. The fire could have been caused by the electrical wires or by spontaneous combustion of film stock. It was the biggest fire in Fort Lee since the Éclair laboratory blaze in 1914. Eventually, all the Fort Lee studios would be destroyed by fire after they had become mere warehouses for the storage of sets from New York theaters when filmmaking stopped in New Jersey. For Capellani, in any case, the destruction of the laboratory was a serious setback. Part of the film footage may have disappeared in the flames, and the studio's productions were severely delayed. Capellani was also having problems with Marjorie Rambeau, who was threatening to sue him because she had not received her salary.[14] However, they reached an amicable out-of-court settlement by mid-January 1920, by which time the shooting of *The Fortune Teller* was completed.

The picture came out in May 1920 with a new distribution company, Robertson-Cole. It would be Capellani's last film as an independent producer. *The Fortune Teller* is the story of Renée Browning (Marjorie Rambeau), who is unjustly accused of adultery by her husband (Frederick Burton). He takes advantage of the accusation to obtain a divorce and to secure the custody of their son, Stephen. Renée becomes a circus fortune teller and an alcoholic. Twenty years later, her son visits the circus to have his fortune told. Realizing his identity, she encourages him. He becomes a renowned politician, and Renée wins back his affection and recovers her dignity. Later, in the 1930s, Marjorie Rambeau (born in 1889) often played the part of an alcoholic old woman—for example, in Frank Borzage's *Man's Castle* (1933).

The Fortune Teller got mixed reviews. While the subject was considered original, the film was too long. *Variety*'s review was typical: "Albert Capellani is the director. He permitted the story to be told in altogether too much footage and this also applies to its progression until 75 minutes are consumed in its unwinding as at present cut. Then it seemed to have suddenly dawned upon him that there was no more precious time to be wasted, so he abruptly ended all further proceedings with a hasty 'clinch.'"[15] Another reviewer discussed the main theme: how mother love was necessary for the development of a child. "This is brought out by [Marjorie Rambeau]'s remarkably fine characterization rather than by Capellani's direction. . . . The direction is capable in detail, but lays too much stress on the unimportant instead of driving steadily along the main line of interest. The entire product is a high class one, and, as shown at the Broadway, it should prove a fine entertainment anywhere."[16] These reviews suggest that the picture may have suffered from the Solax laboratory fire. Maybe footage was lost and not reshot, or shooting was curtailed through lack of funds.

In any case, it was Capellani's swan song as head of his own company. On April 7, 1920, he signed a contract with Cosmopolitan Productions, whose owner was press magnate William Randolph Hearst.

17

Cosmopolitan Productions

People often make fun of William Randolph Hearst's motion-picture productions, mentioning the costly costume dramas or society melodramas he produced for his mistress, Marion Davies. Orson Welles's *Citizen Kane* (1941) reinforced this tale by depicting Marion as vain and talentless (an opera singer in the film). In fact, Marion Davies was a remarkable comedian and played in several masterpieces of silent comedy, such as *The Patsy* (1928) and *Show People* (1928), both directed by King Vidor. Nevertheless, it's true to say that Cosmopolitan did not use Marion Davies's comic talent to the full. However, the company produced some excellent pictures, such as Frank Borzage's *Humoresque* (1920), which made its director a household name.

Capellani's first picture with Cosmopolitan was *The Inside of the Cup* (1921), adapted from a novel by Winston Churchill, an American novelist who became famous before the great British prime minister of the same name. The film was an attack on bigotry and hypocrisy. John Hodder (William P. Carleton) becomes rector of a fashionable church. Banker Eldon Parr (David Torrence) drives his children out of his home by his dishonest conduct. His daughter Alison (Edith Hallor) becomes a settlement worker in the nearby slums. Parr also forbids his son (John Bohn) to marry a salesgirl. Rector Hodder denounces from the pulpit Parr's infamy. Then one of his former employees shoots Parr before committing suicide. The banker repents before dying. This moralizing tale received mixed reviews. *Variety* complained that the picture was a "placid drama, lacking in forceful and gripping movement, interesting only to the point it suggests faithfully a predominating moral, but is much overdrawn. . . . But the story itself is not the best kind of material for a picture, primarily because it sermonizes too much, instead of offering dramatic action in the quantity that a fountain may spout water."[1] On the other hand, another reviewer spoke of a "powerful and picturesque answer, with moments of deep pathos, pure drama in its form and treatment. Notable strength in *The Inside of the Cup* is that of the cast. Almost every member of it is a star. Even the minor roles are so perfectly typed that each one of them assumes a decided significance. . . . *The Inside of the Cup* is packing the Criterion Theatre to overflowing, even at matinees, and it is bound to create a sensation throughout the country."[2]

Although production was finished on June 19, 1920, the film was not released until January 1921. On August 28, 1920, Capellani filed a suit against Cosmopolitan. He had been hired by the company on April 9 and completed his first feature on June 19. However, the company had paid him only $3,000 out of the $20,000 they owed him. His contract stipulated he was to shoot four feature films of 6,000 to 9,000 feet each.[3] Capellani asked for payment; apparently the suit was quickly settled out of court, because on September 28, he was again working for the company on a new feature, *The Wild Goose* (1921).[4] During this time Capellani seemed to be experiencing a whirlwind of financial troubles: on October 1, 1920, his own former company was sued by the U.S. Fidelity & Guaranty Company for $1,065 due on a liability-insurance policy.[5]

In December 1920, Capellani and his family went back to France for a vacation. The stay lasted several months. Was he already thinking of staying for good? If so, he decided against it. The situation of the French studios was no better than it was the year before. Shortly before Capellani's return to New York on April 29, 1921, the trade press announced that he had signed again with Cosmopolitan pictures.[6] He was still mentioned in the most flattering terms, as being "one of the foremost directors of motion pictures in the world."[7] A photograph of Albert accompanying the article showed a tired man who looked much older than his actual age. He was only forty-six.

Unfortunately, more financial troubles were brewing for Capellani. On April 21, 1921, the New Jersey Company sued Albert Capellani Productions for $14,500 alleged to be due as rent for the Solax studios.[8] And Marjorie Rambeau's complaints continued. She asked to be paid for her work on *The Fortune Teller*. She had been hired for six weeks of work at $2,500 per week, but received only five weeks' pay. She won her case in June 1922, getting either $2,712 or $2,835, according to various reports.[9]

Back in New York, Capellani attended the premiere of an important French feature, *J'accuse* (1919), presented to the public by its young director, Abel Gance, who knew Capellani well. In 1912, the young Gance, who was then an unknown actor, was selling film stories to earn a living. He came to see Capellani at Pathé to offer him *Un tragique amour de Mona Lisa* (1912), which Capellani directed. On May 3, 1921, *J'accuse* was presented, in a shortened version, to the VIPs gathered for the occasion in the ballroom of the Ritz-Carlton Hotel in New York. The reviews in the American press were scathing. Gance's ode to pacifism did not conform to America's idea of entertainment. According to one review, "The war picture *J'accuse*, written and directed by Abel Gance, is an unsatisfactory attempt at feature making, which rebounds between the tiresome and the sublime."[10] Gance spoke before the screening to warn the public and the reviewers that the French film industry "had not at [their] disposal your financial and technical facilities."[11] At the screening, Capellani had a chance to discuss with his young colleague the state of filmmaking in France. Gance had just completed *La Roue* (1922), which had suffered an exhausting and troubled shoot riddled by technical and financial problems. Charles Pathé had ceased to support him. The Pathé company had been divided and no longer provided financial support for film production, as Gance discovered during the last weeks of *La Roue*. Capellani must therefore have been told all this and more about the state of the French film industry in 1921.

Toward the end of June 1921, Capellani's last French production was finally released in French theaters. *Quatre-vingt-treize* must have looked prehistoric to a 1920s audience. Motion pictures had undergone a revolution in the years since 1914. One article commented of the film, "It's easy to notice the picture was shot a long time ago and with the makeshift means we had at the time. There are no close-ups, and it's disastrous."[12] Nevertheless, another noted in the defense of the director, "No doubt if Mr. Capellani had shot the picture last year, it would have been perfect."[13] It would take a while before *Quatre-vingt-treize* could be appreciated fully and put into perspective in the history of film. Fortunately, we can also read of its release: "Expected for a very long time—the film was shot before August 1914 and banned by censors during the war!—this beautiful work, which carries the marks of stage traditions of which motion picture was not freed yet, is nevertheless remarkable."[14]

The picture Capellani shot before his holiday in France was finally released on June 5, 1921. *The Wild Goose* (1921) was adapted from a novel by Gouverneur Morris, a best-selling novelist who had been thinking of adapting his own work to the screen as early as July 1919, when Samuel Goldwyn was launching his Eminent Authors' Pictures by recruiting famous writers. But nothing came of that; instead, it fell to Capellani to adapt Morris's story of a love triangle. Ogden Fenn (Norman Kerry) is attracted by Diana (Mary MacLaren), who is married to Frank Manners (Holmes E. Herbert). The latter discovers his wife loves Fenn and decides to avenge himself. But Mrs.

Hastings (Dorothy Bernard), who secretly loves Manners, dissuades him from intervening. In the end, Mr. Hastings kills Fenn by driving his car over a steep embankment. Diana and Frank Manners are finally reconciled.

Variety said, "The name of Capellani guarantees a certain expertness of directorship, and the picture has some splendid examples of fine backgrounds, both out of doors and interiors. The lighting effects are notably fine throughout. . . . Pretty artificial fiction, although it may have a certain appeal to feminine sympathies."[15] *Film Daily* complained about the direction: "Mediocre; has players overacting considerably and dramatic sequences don't register as such."[16] The reviewer added that the public at the Rialto cinema even laughed during a dramatic scene.

Capellani only shot another two pictures. On April 27, 1921, he started working on a Marion Davies film, which would not be seen for fifteen months. Furthermore, the film was cocredited to Roger G. Vignola, who directed several Marion Davies vehicles. It looks as if the film was taken over by Vignola after Capellani's departure.

His other feature, *Sisters* (1922), was again a melodrama adapted from a best-selling novel of the time by Kathleen Norris. It was probably shot after the Marion Davies vehicle, toward the end of 1921, but was released before the Davies film. *Sisters* was produced by the International Film Service Corporation, another Hearst company. The advertising was in the hands of the Hearst press, which syndicated the novel in serial form throughout the country, ensuring a readership of more than 20 million every day. The plot revolved around two sisters. The younger, Cherry (Gladys Leslie), marries Martin Lloyd (Joe King). The elder, Alix (Seena Owen), marries Peter (Matt Moore), who had been in love with Cherry. Unhappy with her marriage, Cherry comes to live with her sister and tries to seduce Peter. The latter is about to elope with her when Alix manages to stop him. The two couples agree to start anew.

If the plot was not particularly original, the reviewers seemed happy with Cappelani's treatment of the story. According to *Variety*, "The picture from the standpoint of story, cast, photography and editing is as good as any that has been seen in Broadway in weeks. It is well acted and the interest, even though the production is seven reels in length, never lags. . . . *Sisters* with a smash of advertising behind it is certain to be a box office winner."[17] *Film Daily*'s reviewer wrote that the film "succeeds in presenting a problem and proving its point—the fallacy of divorce and the sanctity of the marriage vow—in convincing fashion, for one reason, because of splendid restraint on the part of the players."[18]

Capellani's last film released to American screens was a big-budget production starring Marion Davies. *The Young Diana*, adapted from a Marie Corelli novel, offered a story about miraculous rejuvenation, a popular plot device of the time, used in such pictures as Frank Lloyd's *Black Oxen* (1924), in which Corinne Griffith manages to stay eternally young thanks to a mysterious medical treatment. It's difficult to ascertain Capellani's input in the picture compared with that of codirector Roger G. Vignola, who was Davies's regular director at the time. It may be that the picture was reshot: Capellani started filming toward the end of April 1921, but the film was not released until August 1922. When it came out, Capellani had already left Cosmopolitan for good. Indeed, in January 1922 the trade press mentioned that Capellani was about to start the shooting of *Enemies of Women*, an adaptation of a Vicente Blasco-Ibáñez novel, the world-famous author of *The Four Horsemen of the Apocalypse* (1921), already filmed by Rex Ingram. But on February 27, 1922, the production of *Enemies of Women* was suspended indefinitely. And by May 10, Roger Vignola had taken over the direction. In the end, Alan Crosland directed it and the picture did not come out until September 1923.

The Young Diana tells the story of Diana May (Marion

Davies), who becomes a bitter, sad spinster after losing the sweetheart of her youth, Richard Cleeve (Forrest Stanley). Twenty years later, Dr. Dimitrius (Pedro de Cordoba) restores her youth and beauty, thanks to an elixir of youth. She meets Cleeve again, who is now married, and spurns his advances. Then Diana awakens and realizes it was only a dream. She is reunited with Cleeve and lives happily ever after.

The art director, Joseph Urban, offered lavish settings—no expense was spared in this production. Urban was then a famous set designer, working for the Ziegfeld Follies and the Metropolitan Opera House. Davies wore an unusual number of gowns, as was often the case in Cosmopolitan productions. *Variety* wrote a rave review of this glossy feature: "Miss Davies in *The Young Diana* plays with poise, surety and splendid artistry. In the transition from Youth to Age she surpasses the finer moments of Mary Pickford in *Stella Maris*. Diana is her best role unequivocally. . . . With its superb photography, sumptuous settings and regal costuming *The Young Diana* shines forth one of the real regular releases of the year."[19] Others were not convinced by this overlong and overdressed production. "The directors have procured some good results, but the production as a whole is stretched beyond capacity and not over convincing. It is almost entirely studio stuff, and while it has a good many romantic and mystic qualities, it is handled in a very realistic manner. . . . The directors have done some very good work in handling a small but effective cast, but they have allowed a little over-acting on the part of the star and have also allowed her to divert the attention from the story to her many curious gowns."[20]

After the release of *The Young Diana*, Capellani disappeared from the trade press, except for a few fugitive mentions. Just before leaving America for good, he met Ben Carré, the art director who had worked on Capellani's first American productions at World. Carré had just come back from California after a stint with Marshall Neilan. He got in touch with Henri

Ménessier, who told him where to find Capellani. Carré went to the Hearst studios in New York, where Capellani had just completed his last feature. Albert told Carré that his family had already gone back to France and he was on the verge of leaving himself. The two walked around the set of *When Knighthood Was in Flower* (1922), another Marion Davies vehicle directed by Roger Vignola, which was being shot in the spring of 1922. Carré got the impression that Capellani's return to France would be only temporary.[21] It is quite possible that Capellani was only thinking of a holiday. But he would not return to the United States. It may be that his deteriorating health after seven years of intensive work had exhausted him. The exact date of his return to France is unknown, but it must have been in the summer of 1922. His American adventure was over.

18

Back Home

Returning home after seven years abroad must have been extremely difficult. When Capellani received journalist Alfred Bonneau from *Cinémagazine* in April 1923, the journalist noticed that Albert had drastically altered his appearance: he had shaved his famous beard. Capellani even had difficulty finding a flat in Paris and was now living at 156 Boulevard Pereire in the 17th arrondissement. It was a return to his roots in the district of his youth—though he was not in the middle-class area of Les Batignolles, but in the more affluent one of Les Ternes.

As for any future projects, he told Bonneau, "When I came back to Paris, I was thinking of retiring and getting a rest, but inactivity weighs heavily on me. And soon, if the talks I'm about to start are successful, I'll have the joy to work again in my country after eight years away."[1] The project Capellani had in mind was related to the Victorine studios in Nice.

The situation of the film industry in France needs to be clarified here. In 1920, Charles Pathé ceased film production altogether, preserving only his film stock factory. A few months later, banker Denis Ricaud gathered a few investors to create a new distribution company, Pathé-Consortium-Cinéma, in the process acquiring Pathé-Cinéma. By autumn 1921, Ricaud was expelled from the board, accused of financial mismanagement. Then Ricaud tried to acquire the Victorine studios in Nice. This was where Capellani became involved in the project. Victorine, then called Ciné-Studios, was a fairly modern facility, though not up to contemporary American standards. Its owner-producer, Serge Sandberg, did not intend to sell.

However, one of the main shareholders of the studio, Jules Schréter, asked Alice Guy-Blaché to write a report regarding the studio's potential, as he was interested in selling his shares. This assignment must have been a godsend for a destitute Alice, who had returned to France in 1922, unknown and forgotten. In September 1922, she started inquiring about Victorine and met a number of producers who might be interested in renting the studio. As Capellani and Alice had been close friends for years, she was able to tell him everything about the place, though the report was confidential.

In July 1923, Capellani and Ricaud took the train to Nice to visit the studio. An employee there, a Mr. Dauny, showed them the place. He became upset when he realized that his visitors were so well informed and wrote to his superior immediately after the tour:

> Mr. Ricaud, accompanied by Mr. Capellani, arrived indeed in Nice last Friday at 1:30 p.m. and, following your instructions, I went to meet them at the Ruhl Hotel to drive them immediately to La Victorine. I had the impression that these men were well informed about *everything*. Actually, I learned later that M. Capellani is intimate with a Mme. Blaché, who came to see you last year, recommended by M. Bottin and M. Schréter, when they wanted to make something out of Ciné-Studio. This person (Mme. Blaché) obviously had access to all the useful documents; she even went to England in order to find clients for us. She simply told Capellani everything she knew, i.e., the price paid for La Victorine, the mortgages (which I wasn't even aware of), etc. Nevertheless, these gentlemen visited the building meticulously, in terms of real estate as well as technically, and I don't think their impression was unfavorable, while they can still invoke insufficient facilities (especially the electrical ones, etc.). In addi-

tion, M. Ricaud and M. Capellani *inquired* all over town. They were told that the land, considering its vicinity with the cemetery, wasn't worth more than 15 or 20 francs per square meter![2]

After the visit, Ricaud considered purchasing La Victorine, together with a British company, in order to create a Franco-British consortium. But the deal never materialized; Sandberg did not want to part with the studio. Capellani must have been mortified. This wonderful opportunity to work in the best studio then available in France vanished. It shows also that he was not aware of the complex power struggle between Schréter, Ricaud, and Sandberg; neither was Alice Guy-Blaché when she wrote her report.

Some years passed; in 1927, the press mentioned that "Albert Capellani, one of the most senior French directors, is coming back to directing after a three-year rest [*sic*]. He is working on the continuity of *Werther*."[3] This adaptation of Goethe's novel did not materialize, either.

Meanwhile, Albert's brother Paul, back in France since 1919, gave an interview in 1929 in which he stated, "My brother was compelled to give up his activity as director which he loved so much because of his health."[4] While Paul's relationship with his brother was then strained, he must have been well aware of Albert's health problems. Albert Capellani was now retired for good. Years went by without any change in his situation. Nevertheless, the Capellani name returned to theater marquees thanks to his son, Roger. The young Capellani started as a film editor and became a director at the start of the talkies in the early thirties.

We know little about Capellani's last years. According to his grandson, his health deteriorated. He had difficulties coping with his forced inactivity and his physical state. It appears he suffered a stroke, a typical side effect for untreated diabetics who suffer from high blood pressure. His loss of mobility made him even more irritable.

He hardly ever saw his brother Paul, with whom he had severed all contact. Paul was now living with their mother, Valérie-Anna, in the 8th arrondissement at 44 Rue de Moscou since his return to France. At the age of fifty, on December 24, 1927, Paul married for the first time. His wife was Marie-Léonie Bürckel, age fifty-seven, whom Paul had known for many years. His mother came to the wedding, but Albert did not. Paul worked on the stage until 1930, when he was diagnosed with a heart problem and was advised to retire to the sun. He left Paris for Cagnes-sur-mer, where he would live until his death, practicing his first love, sculpture.

Albert died on September 26, 1931, at his home in Boulevard Pereire. His death was hardly mentioned in the press of the time; by then he was virtually forgotten. There was just a brief article in *Cinéopse:* "The whole of the film industry was hit hard by the announcement of Albert Capellani's death, a pioneer of the heroic early days, struck down by an attack of paralysis, whose funeral took place on Monday, September 28, strictly in private."[5]

His mother, Valérie-Anna, died in 1937, having survived the death of four of her own children. As for Paul, he passed away on November 7, 1960, at the age of eighty-three, in La Capelle, his house in Cagnes-sur-mer.

There is a tragic epilogue in the Capellani family story. As if history was repeating itself, Albert's son, Roger Capellani, died in Zuydcoote on May 30, 1940, during the Dunkirk retreat as French and British troops were stuck on the coast facing the German offensive. Like his uncle Maurice, he gave his life for his country. Roger's premature death at the age of thirty-five marked the end of moviemaking in the Capellani family.

Albert Capellani's memory was put on ice for many years. His widow, Léonie-Marie, refused to mention his film career, and the family archives disappeared. His French films became only vague memories, and his American ones fared no better.

The sound era destroyed any remembrance of his works, which were obsolete and forgotten.

For years, film historians attached little importance to Capellani. Eventually, however, he came back into favor, thanks to the restoration of some of his French masterpieces such as *Germinal* and *Quatre-vingt-treize* (whose merits were often ascribed incorrectly to André Antoine) in the 1980s. Over the past fifteen years his grandson Bernard Basset-Capellani (Simonne's son) has done all he could to gather information on his grandfather and to promote his work.

Capellani's real renaissance took place in 2010 and 2011 during Bologna's Cinema Ritrovato film festival, where Mariann Lewinsky curated for the first time a retrospective of Capellani's French and American films. There is still a lot of work to do to find and restore all the French and American silents that are still extant in various formats and fragments. Fortunately, the interest in his work will now not wane. Film historian Kristin Thompson summed up Capellani's position following the Bologna retrospective: "Those festival guests who missed the Capellani films missed, in my opinion, the rewriting of early film history. He is not simply another important silent filmmaker to be placed in the pantheon. Film by film, this year and last, I kept comparing what I was watching with what D. W. Griffith had made that same year. In each case, Capellani's film seemed more sophisticated, more engaging, and more polished." And she concludes, "With the end of the main retrospective, however, it is safe to say that from now on anyone who claims to know early film history will need to be familiar with Capellani's work."[6]

Acknowledgments

I am indebted to the following people who helped me in various degrees in my research for this biography of Albert Capellani. For their help I wish to thank Bernard Basset-Capellani, Michèle Bertaux from the Maison de Victor Hugo Museum, Lenny Borger, Guy Borlée from Cineteca di Bologna, Serge Bromberg from Lobster Films, Kevin Brownlow, Bryony Dixon from the British Film Institute, Phoebe Green, Valdo Kneubühler from Cinémathèque française, Stéphane Launey, Mariann Lewinsky, Stéphanie Salmon from the Fondation Jérôme Seydoux-Pathé, Sophie Seydoux from the Fondation Jérôme Seydoux-Pathé, Fernando Silva Astorga, Jay Weissberg, and Eléonore Winkler from Lobster Films.

I also would like to thank the staff of the Bibliothèque nationale de France (BnF), of the Bibliothèque du Film (BiFi), of the Vincennes city archives, of the Paris Archives, and of the British Film Institute.

Filmography

Compiled with Mariann Lewinsky

<u>Underlining</u> of a film title indicates that a print or fragment is extant. Working titles appear in parentheses. An asterisk indicates that a film is available on DVD. "SCAGL" means that the film was produced by the Société Cinématographique des Auteurs et Gens de Lettres.

In France[1]

1905

Le Prestidigitateur pratique[2]
July 1905
Scene with special effects, 40 m

<u>*Le Chemineau*</u> *
December 1905
Dramatic scene, 110 m

1906

La Voix de la conscience
February 1906
Dramatic scene, 85 m

<u>*Drame passionnel*</u> *
April–May 1906
Dramatic scene, 125 m

<u>*La Loi du pardon*</u> *
April–May 1906
Dramatic scene, 145 m

*Mortelle idylle**
August 1906
Dramatic scene, 105 m

*La Fille du sonneur**
September 1906
Dramatic scene, 235 m
With Gabriel Moreau, René Coge, and little Ransart

*Pauvre mère**
September 1906
Dramatic scene, 115 m

*L'Âge du cœur**
October 1906
Dramatic scene, 85 m

*La Femme du lutteur**
October 1906
Dramatic scene, 150 m

*Aladin ou la lampe merveilleuse**
October 1906
Fairy tale, 250 m
With Georges Vinter

1907

*Cendrillon ou la pantoufle merveilleuse**
January 1907
Fairy tale, 295 m

*Les Deux sœurs**
April 1907
Dramatic scene, 225 m

Les Apprentissages de Boireau
May 1907
Comedy, 205 m
With André Deed and Aurèle Sidney

Amour d'esclave *
May 1907
Dramatic scene, 210 m
With Gabriel Moreau and Darenne Bennard

La Légende de Polichinelle
June 1907
Fairy tale, 410 m
With Max Linder

La Fille du bûcheron
June 1907
Dramatic scene, 185 m

Not' fanfare concourt
August 1907
Comedy, 195 m
With André Deed

Le Pied de mouton *
November 1907
Fairy tale, 300 m

1908

La belle au bois dormant (Capellani and/or Lucien Nonguet)
March 1908
Fairy tale, 300 m

La Vestale
March 1908
Dramatic scene, 225 m

Don Juan
May 1908
Dramatic scene, 330 m

Béatrix Cenci
June 1908
Dramatic scene, 225 m

Samson
June 1908
Biblical scene, 330 m

Riquet à la houppe
July 1908
Fairy tale, 290 m
With Georges Monca

Le Foulard merveilleux
July 1908
Scene with special effects, 145 m
With André Deed and Aurèle Sidney

Le Chat botté
August 1908
Fairy tale, 225 m

La Belle et la Bête * (fragment)
August 1908
Fairy tale, 190 m

Peau d'âne
September 1908
Fairy tale, 310 m

Corso Tragique[3]
September 1908
Dramatic scene, 240 m

Marie Stuart *
September 1908
Historical scene, 255 m
With Jeanne Delvair, Jacques Grétillat, Henry-Krauss, and
Paul Capellani

L'Arlésienne * SCAGL
October 1908
Dramatic scene, 355 m
With Jeanne Grumbach, Henri Desfontaines, and Jean-Marié
de l'Isle

L'Homme aux gants blancs * SCAGL
December 1908
Dramatic scene, 310 m
With Marguerite Brésil, Jacques Grétillat, and Henri
Desfontaines

1909

L'Assommoir * SCAGL
April 1909
Dramatic scene, 740 m
With Eugénie Nau, Jacques Grétillat, Catherine Fonteney,
and Alexandre Arquillères

Le Roi s'amuse SCAGL
August 1909
Dramatic scene, 350 m
With Henri Sylvain, Paul Capellani, and Marcelle Géniat

La Mort du Duc d'Enghien en 1804* SCAGL
November 1909
Historical scene, 310 m
With Georges Grand and Germaine Dermoz

Le Luthier de Crémone
November 1909
Miscellaneous scene, 235 m
With Amélie Diéterle and Jean Dax

Les Deux orphelines SCAGL (also attributed to Georges Monca)
December 1909
Dramatic scene, 355 m
With Gabrielle Rosny and Georges Dorival

1910

La Zingara
April 1910
Dramatic scene, 210 m
With Stacia Napierkowska

Sous la Terreur SCAGL
May 1910
Dramatic scene, 280 m

La Mariée du Château maudit (*La Fiancée du château maudit*) SCAGL
June 1910

Dramatic scene, 255 m
With Carmen Deraisy and Victor Capoul

Fra Diavolo SCAGL
July 1910
Dramatic scene, 245 m
With Jean Angelo and Eugénie Nau

La Bouteille de lait SCAGL
July 1910
Comedy-drama, 295 m
With Henri Etiévant and Alphonse Dieudonné

La Puissance du souvenir (*Le Monstre*) SCAGL
August 1910
Dramatic scene, 230 m
With André Hall and Régina Sandri

L'Honneur (*Pour l'honneur*) SCAGL
October 1910
Dramatic scene, 405 m
With Georges Grand, Armand Bour, and Georges Saillard

La Vengeance de la morte (*Le Portrait*) SCAGL
October 1910
Dramatic scene, 210 m
With Paul Capellani and Jeanne Bérangère

La Victime de Sophie (*Victime de l'amour*) SCAGL
October 1910
Comedy, 175 m
With Emile Milo, Armand Numès, and Regina Sandri

Le Voile du bonheur SCAGL
November 1910
Dramatic scene, 365 m
With Henry-Krauss and Henri Etiévant

L'Evadé des Tuileries (*Une journée de la Révolution*) SCAGL
November 1910
Historical scene, 320 m
With Gabrielle Robinne and Georges Grand

La Complice (*L'Echarpe*) SCAGL
December 1910
Dramatic scene, 255 m
With Stacia Napierkowska, Paul Numa, and Fernand
Tauffenberger

Le Spoliateur (*L'autre "un drame en wagon"*) SCAGL
December 1910
Dramatic scene, 290 m
With Paul Capellani and Maurice Luguet

Fâcheuse méprise[4] SCAGL
Shooting: 20–22 July 1910
With Emile Milo and Jean Dax

1911

Le Roman de la momie (*La Momie*) SCAGL
January 1911
Dramatic scene, 250 m
With Paul Franck and Romuald Joubé

Péché de jeunesse (*Le Roman d'un jour*) SCAGL
February 1911
Dramatic scene, 330 m
With Georges Grand and Gabrielle Robinne

Amour de page SCAGL[5]
February 1911
Fairy tale, 225 m
With Victor Capoul and Gabrielle Robinne

L'Intrigante * (*L'Institutrice*) SCAGL
March 1911
Comedy-drama, 175 m
With Georges Coquet and Catherine Fonteney

L'Envieuse (*Le Vol*) SCAGL
March 1911
Dramatic scene, 285 m
With Adolphe Candé, Léontine Massart, and Maurice Luguet

La Mauvaise intention (*L'Image*) SCAGL
March 1911
Dramatic scene, 255 m
With Charles Mosnier, Renée Sylvaire, and Georges Le Roy

Le Prix de vertu SCAGL
March 1911
Comedy, 255 m
With Germaine Reuver, Georges Tréville, and Bach

L'Epouvante * (*Le coucher d'une étoile*) SCAGL
April 1911
Dramatic scene, 235 m
With Emile Milo and Mistinguett

La Danseuse de Siva SCAGL
April 1911
Dramatic scene, 285 m
With Stacia Napierkowska, Georges Tréville, and Emile Milo

Le Rideau noir SCAGL
April 1911
Dramatic scene, 250 m
With Paul Capellani, Jacques Grétillat, and Germaine Dermoz

Les Deux collègues SCAGL
April 1911
Comedy, 160 m
With André Simon and Paul Calvin

La Poupée de l'orpheline (*La Poupée brisée*) SCAGL
May 1911
Dramatic scene, 215 m
With Mévisto, Eugénie Nau, and Maria Fromet

Les Deux chemins (*Les Deux sœurs*) SCAGL
May 1911
Comedy-drama, 290 m
With Jacques Grétillat and Mistinguett

*Le Pain des petits oiseaux** SCAGL
May 1911
Comedy-drama, 265 m
With Stacia Napierkowska and Edmond Duquesne

Le Courrier de Lyon ou l'attaque de la malle-poste SCAGL
May 1911
Dramatic scene, 780 m
With Louis Ravet, Mévisto, Alphonse Dieudonné,[6] and Paul Capellani

Jacintha la Cabaretière (*Les émotions de Jacintha*) SCAGL
June 1911
Dramatic scene, 260 m
With Paul Capellani, Lucie Pacitti, and Georges Tréville

Un Monsieur qui a un tic SCAGL
June 1911
Comedy, 165 m
With Mévisto, Maurice Luguet, and Madeleine Guitty

Par respect de l'enfant (*Le Sacrifice*) SCAGL
June 1911
Dramatic scene, 295 m
With Paul Capellani, Georges Tréville, Emile Milo, and
Jeanne Bérangère

Pour voir Paris[7]
July 1911
Comedy, 300 m
With Charles Lorrain and Suzanne Goldstein

Deux filles d'Espagne (*Deux jeunes filles se ressemblent*) SCAGL
July 1911
Comedy-drama, 195 m
With Emile Milo, Charles Deschamps, and La California

L'Oiseau s'envole SCAGL
August 1911
Comedy, 285 m
With Henry-Krauss, Suzanne Goldstein, and Eugénie Nau

Le Mémorial de Sainte Hélène ou la captivité de Napoléon[8]
SCAGL
August 1911
Historical scene, 610 m
With Laroche, Georges Tréville, and Emile Milo

La Vision de frère Benoît (*Frère Benoît*)
September 1911
Religious scene, 215 m
With Georges Tréville and Mévisto

Notre-Dame de Paris SCAGL
September 1911
Dramatic scene, 810 m
With Henry-Krauss, Stacia Napierkowska, and Claude Garry

Le Visiteur SCAGL
October 1911
Dramatic scene, 295 m
With Polaire and Georges Tréville

Ducroquet a volé la Joconde (*Gribouille a volé la Joconde*)
(Capellani and G. Denola)[9]
November 1911
Comedy, 170 m

Les Six petits tambours (1794) SCAGL
November 1911
Dramatic scene, 285 m
With Jean Kemm

Robert Bruce, épisode des guerres de l'indépendance écossaise
SCAGL
November 1911
Historical scene, 405 m
With Paul Capellani, Louis Ravet, and Henri Etiévant

Les Aventures de Cyrano de Bergerac SCAGL
December 1911
Heroic comedy, 735 m
With Emile Milo, Paul Capellani, Henri Etiévant, and Andrée
Pascal

Rabastens SCAGL[10]
Shooting: July and September 1911

1912

La Bohème SCAGL
February 1912
Dramatic scene, 770 m
With Paul Capellani, Suzanne Revonne, and Charles
Dechamps

La Fin de Robespierre (*La Dernière charrette*) SCAGL
(fragment)
February 1912
Historical scene, 425 m
With Georges Saillard, Jacques Grétillat, and Marie Ventura

La Vengeance de Licinius[11]
February 1912
Dramatic scene, 285 m
With Henri Etiévant, Impéria, and Georges Tréville

Un Amour de la du Barry
April 1912
Dramatic scene, 390 m
With Stacia Napierkowska and Henry-Krauss

Un Tragique amour de Mona Lisa (*La Joconde*) SCAGL
April 1912
Dramatic scene, 550 m
With Claude Garry, Jacques Grétillat, and Aimée Raynal

Le Congrès des balayeurs (*Le Congrès des maires*) SCAGL
April 1912
Comedy, 240 m
With Henri Collen

Filmography

Milord l'Arsouille [12]
June 1912
Historical scene, 460 m
With Stacia Napierkowska and Castillan

Les Mystères de Paris SCAGL
July 1912
Dramatic scene, 1,540 m
With Paul Capellani, Henri Etiévant, Eugénie Nau, and
Jeanne Delvair

Josette SCAGL
July 1912
Dramatic scene, 385 m
With Paul Capellani, Georges Dorival, and Paule Andrale

La Bien aimée (*Douce Alsace*) SCAGL [13]
September 1912
Dramatic scene, 805 m
With Stacia Napierkowska and Jean Angelo

Le Signalement SCAGL
October 1912
Dramatic scene, 310 m
With Jean Kemm and Marie Fromet

Les Misérables SCAGL
November 1912
3,445 m (in 4 episodes)
With Henry-Krauss, Marie Ventura, Henri Etiévant, and
Mistinguett

1913

Le Nabab SCAGL
April 1913
Dramatic scene, 1,130 m
With Léon Bernard, Jean Dax, and Mévisto

L'Absent SCAGL
May 1913
Comedy of Dutch customs, 830 m
With Henri Etiévant, Henri Rollan, Jeanne Grumbach, and
Germaine Dermoz

Le Rêve interdit SCAGL
May 1913
Comedy, 705 m
With Gabriel de Gravone, Georges Saillard, and Suzanne
Revonne

Germinal * SCAGL
October 1913
Dramatic scene, 3,020 m
With Henry-Krauss, Sylvie, Jean Jacquinet, and Mévisto

La Glu SCAGL
November 1913
Dramatic scene, 1,900 m
With Henry-Krauss, Paul Capellani, and Mistinguett

1914

Le Chevalier de Maison-Rouge * SCAGL
February 1914
Historical scene, 2,265 m
With Léa Piron, Marie-Louise Derval, Paul Escoffier,
Mévisto, and Henri Rollan

La Guerre du feu SCAGL (Capellani and G. Denola)[14]
February 1914
Dramatic scene, 490 m
With Georges Dorival

La Belle limonadière SCAGL (Capellani and Adrien Caillard)[15]
July 1914
Dramatic scene, 1,605 m
With Marie-Louise Derval and Jean Jacquinet

Films shot in 1914, but released later

1917

Marie Tudor SCAGL
Dramatic scene, 1,600 m
With Jeanne Delvair, Paul Capellani, and Romuald Joubé

Patrie SCAGL
Dramatic scene, 1,885 m
With Henry-Krauss, Paul Capellani, and Yvonne Sergyl

1921

Quatre-vingt-treize * SCAGL
June 1921
Historical scene, 2,820 m
With Henry-Krauss, Paul Capellani, and Philippe Garnier

In the United States[16]

1915

The Face in the Moonlight (World Film Corporation)
Writer: Anthony Paul Kelly; photography: Lucien Andriot; art direction: Ben Carré[17]
With Robert Warwick, Stella Archer, and Montagu Love

The Impostor (World Film Corporation)
Writer: E. M. Ingleton; photography: Lucien Andriot
With Jose Collins, Alec B. Francis, and Leslie Stowe

The Flash of an Emerald (World Film Corporation) (one reel)
Writer: Captain Leslie T. Peacocke; photography: David Calcagni
With Robert Warwick and Dorothy Fairchild

Camille (World Film Corporation)
Writer: Frances Marion; photography: Lucien Andriot
With Clara Kimball Young, Paul Capellani, and Robert Cummings

1916

The Feast of Life (World Film Corporation)
Writer: Frances Marion; photography: Lucien Andriot
With Clara Kimball Young, Paul Capellani, Doris Kenyon, and Robert Frazer

La Vie de Bohème (World Film Corporation)
Writer: Frances Marion; photography: Lucien Andriot; art direction: Ben Carré
With Alice Brady, Paul Capellani, and Zeena Keefe

The Dark Silence (World Film Corporation)
Writer: Gardner Hunting; photography: Hal Young
With Clara Kimball Young, Paul Capellani, and Edward T. Langford

The Common Law (Clara Kimball Young Film Corp./Selznick Pictures Corp.)
Writer: Beryl Morhange; photography: Hal Young and Jacques Montéran

With Clara Kimball Young, Conway Tearle, and Paul
Capellani

The Foolish Virgin (Clara Kimball Young Film Corp./Selznick
Pictures Corp.)
Writer: Albert Capellani; photography: Hal Young, George
Peters, and Jacques Montéran
With Clara Kimball Young, Conway Tearle, and Paul
Capellani

1917

The Easiest Way (Clara Kimball Young Film Corp./Selznick
Pictures Corp.)
Writers: Albert Capellani and Frederic Chapin; photography:
Hal Young and Jacques Montéran
With Clara Kimball Young, Joseph Kilgour, and Rockcliffe
Fellowes

American Maid (Mutual Film Corporation)
Writer: Hamilton Smith; photography: David Calcagni
With Edna Goodrich, William B. Davidson, and George
Henry

1918

Daybreak (Metro Pictures Corporation)
Writers: June Mathis and Albert Capellani; photography:
David Calcagni
With Emily Stevens, Julian L'Estrange, and Herman Lieb

Social Hypocrites (Metro Pictures Corporation)
Writers: June Mathis and Albert Capellani; photography:
Eugene Gaudio; art direction: Edward J. Shulter
With May Allison, Frank Currier, Joseph Kilgour, and Henry
Kolker

The Richest Girl (Empire All Star Corp./Mutual Film Corp.)
Writer: Harry R. Durant; photography: Tony Gaudio; art
direction: Henri Ménessier
With Ann Murdock, David Powell, Paul Capellani, and
Gladys Wilson

<u>*The House of Mirth*</u> (Metro Pictures Corporation) (200 m
fragment)
Writers: June Mathis and Albert Capellani; photography:
Eugene Gaudio; art direction: Henri Ménessier
With Katherine Harris Barrymore, Henry Kolker, Christine
Mayo, and Joseph Kilgour

A Woman of France (Metro Pictures Corporation)
Short film with Alla Nazimova to promote Liberty Loans.

<u>*Eye for Eye*</u> (Metro Pictures Corporation) (two reels)
Writers: June Mathis and Albert Capellani; photography:
Eugene Gaudio; art direction: Henri Ménessier
With Alla Nazimova, Charles Bryant, and Sally Crute

1919

Out of the Fog (Metro Pictures Corporation)
Writers: June Mathis and Albert Capellani; photography:
Eugene Gaudio and Eugene Morin; art direction: Henri
Ménessier
With Alla Nazimova, Charles Bryant, and Henry Harman

<u>*The Red Lantern*</u> * (Metro Pictures Corporation)
Writers: June Mathis and Albert Capellani; photography:
Eugene Gaudio; art direction: Henri Ménessier
With Alla Nazimova, Frank Currier, Darrel Foss, and Noah
Beery

Oh, Boy! (Albert Capellani Productions)
Writer: Albert Capellani; photography: Lucien Andriot
With June Caprice, Creighton Hale, and Flora Finch

The Virtuous Model (Albert Capellani Productions)
Writer: Albert Capellani; photography: Lucien Andriot; art
direction: Henri Ménessier
With Dolores Cassinelli, Vincent Serrano, and Franklyn
Farnum

1920

The Fortune Teller (Albert Capellani Productions)
Writer: George Dubois Proctor; photography: Jacques
Montéran; art direction: John D. Braddon
With Marjorie Rambeau, Frederick Burton, and Raymond
McKee

1921

The Inside of the Cup (Cosmopolitan Productions)
Writers: Albert Capellani and George Dubois Proctor;
photography: Al Siegler
With William P. Carleton, David Torrence, Edith Hallor, and
John Bohn

The Wild Goose (Cosmopolitan Productions)
Writer: Donnah Darrell; photography: Harold Westrom; art
direction: Joseph Urban
With Mary MacLaren, Holmes E. Herbert, and Norman
Kerry

1922

Sisters (International Film Service)
Writer: E. Lloyd Sheldon; photography: Chester Lyons; art
direction: Joseph Urban
With Seena Owen, Gladys Leslie, and Matt Moore

The Young Diana (Cosmopolitan Productions)
Writer: Luther Reed; photography: Harold Westrom; art
direction: Joseph Urban
With Marion Davies, Forrest Stanley, and Pedro de Cordoba

As Screenwriter

The Parisian Tigress (1919) directed by Herbert Blaché

As Producer and Supervisor
(Albert Capellani Productions)

The Love Cheat (1919) directed by George Archainbaud
A Damsel in Distress (1919) directed by George Archainbaud
The Right to Lie (1919) directed by Edwin Carewe
In Walked Mary (1920) directed by George Archainbaud

Albert Capellani Films on DVD

Albert Capellani Box—Pathé (4 DVDs): *L'Assommoir, Germinal, Le Chevalier de Maison-Rouge, Quatre-vingt-treize, Drame passionnel, Mortelle idylle, Pauvre mère, La Fille du sonneur, La Femme du lutteur, L'Âge du cœur, Aladin ou la lampe merveilleuse.*

Albert Capellani—Un cinema di grandeur, 1905–1911—Cineteca di Bologna (1 DVD): *L'Épouvante, Le Pain des petits oiseaux, L'Intrigante, L'Homme aux gants blancs, Les Deux sœurs, La Loi du pardon, Le Chemineau, Le Pied de mouton, Cendrillon, Amour d'esclave, L'Arlésienne, La Mort du Duc d'Enghien en 1804, la Belle et la Bête, Marie Stuart.*

The Red Lantern (1919, Albert Capellani), Cinematek—VDFC (1 DVD plus 200-page book).

Peau d'âne (1908, A. Capellani) is available as a featurette on Jacques Demy's *Peau d'âne* (Arte DVD).

The following films are available on the Gaumont-Pathé Archives website: *Drame Passionnel, La Loi du pardon, L'Âge du cœur, Mortelle idylle, La Fille du sonneur, Pauvre mère, La Femme du lutteur, Aladin ou la lampe merveilleuse, Cendrillon ou la pantoufle merveilleuse, Les Apprentissages de Boireau, Amour d'esclave, Le Pied de mouton, La Belle au bois dormant, La Vestale, Béatrix Cenci, Peau d'âne, L'Assommoir, La Mort du Duc d'Enghien en 1804, L'Evadé des Tuileries, Le Courrier de Lyon ou l'attaque de la malle-poste, La Bohème, Les Misérables, L'Absent, Germinal, La Glu, Le Chevalier de Maison-Rouge.*

Notes

Introduction

1. In a letter dated November 24, 1910, Mr. A. Boudier, the secretary of La Société Cinématographique des Auteurs et Gens de Lettres (SCAGL), asked Georges Fagot to hyphenate the name "Henry-Krauss" for "orthographic affinity." Georges Sadoul Papers, Bibliothèque du Film, Paris (hereafter BiFi).

1. From the Marais to the Batignolles

1. Translation by Phoebe Green. Bernard Basset-Capellani Collection.

2. Contrary to what Jean Mitry wrote, Maurice Tourneur was not born in the Belleville district (10th arrondissement) but in the Epinettes district (17th arrondissement) of Paris, Villa Compoint. His father was a manufacturer and wholesaler of imitation jewelry.

2. From Vincennes to the Alhambra

1. Sylvie went on to play Catherine Maheu in *Germinal* (1913). Garry played Claude Frollo in *Notre-Dame de Paris* (1911). He was also the uncle of actor Pierre Fresnay.

2. *Le Petit Parisien,* July 25, 1901, 3.

3. Nadar portrait, ref. NA238 18636 (register 238.3), Musée de l'architecture et du patrimoine, Paris.

4. The address given for Capellani's stay in central London is Guilford Place.

5. *Moving Picture World,* April 24, 1915, 541. Ben Carré says in his memoirs that Capellani was unable to speak English properly when he arrived in the United States in 1915; he needed a translator.

6. Charles Ford, *Albert Capellani précurseur méconnu* (Bois d'Arcy: Services des archives du Film, 1984).

7. Pierre Trimbach, *Quand on tournait la manivelle . . . il y a 60 ans . . . ou les mémoires d'un opérateur de la Belle Epoque* (Paris: CEFAG, 1970), 15.

8. The year 1902 corresponds to Paul's military service; he must have obtained a deferment to perform in the play. Press cuttings in his personal papers confirm his participation.

9. André Antoine, *Mes souvenirs sur le Théâtre Antoine et sur l'Odéon* (Paris: Grasset, 1928).

10. Manuscripts, département des arts du spectacle, Bibliothèque nationale de France, Paris (hereafter BnF).

11. Letter from Paul Capellani to André Antoine, December 5, 1922, Antoine papers, BnF.

12. Commission de Recherche Historique (Historical Research Committee), February 7, 1948, BiFi.

3. Pathé

1. Hughes Laurent, "Souvenirs de 50 ans ! . . . ," *Bulletin de l'Association Française des Ingénieurs et Techniciens du cinéma*, 1957, no. 16, 8.

2. *Pathé-Journal*, no. 5, 1912.

3. *Cinémagazine*, April 20, 1923, 112.

4. Pierre Trimbach, *Quand on tournait la manivelle . . . il y a 60 ans . . . ou les mémoires d'un opérateur de la Belle Epoque* (Paris: CEFAG, 1970), 15. Dating in Trimbach's book is unreliable. For example, he mentions a lunch with Albert Capellani and his father, Charles, in 1908. Yet Charles died in 1902.

5. *L'image*, no. 13, June 10, 1932, 28.

6. Ibid., 29.

7. *L'image*, no. 30, October 7, 1932, 28.

8. Ibid., 29.

9. *La Cinématographie française*, January 20, 1923.

10. *L'image*, no. 9, May 13, 1932, 13.

11. *Cinémagazine 1930* (facsimile edition) (Paris: L'Avant-Scène Cinéma, 1983), 28.

4. The Société Cinématographique des Auteurs et Gens de Lettres

1. Letter from Georges Merzbach to Gustave Simon, March 10, 1908, Maison de Victor Hugo Museum, Paris.

2. Letter from Pierre Decourcelle to Gustave Simon, March 10, 1908, Maison de Victor Hugo Museum, Paris.

3. Letter from the Sons of Bernard Merzbach to Gustave Simon, June 17, 1908, Maison de Victor Hugo Museum, Paris.

4. Letter from Decourcelle to Simon, June 19, 1908, Maison de Victor Hugo Museum, Paris.

5. Letter from A. Boudier to the Prefect, June 22, 1914, Georges Sadoul papers, BiFi.

6. *Cinémagazine 1930* (facsimile edition) (Paris: L'Avant-Scène Cinéma, 1983), 28.

7. SCAGL register, BiFi.

8. Fonteney is still famous for her impersonation of Mrs. Lepic in Julien Duvivier's *Poil de carotte* (1932).

9. Paul Adolphe Tabutiaux (1876–1952) started as a film extra and went on to a very long career in motion pictures. In the 1930s, he was still working for Pathé-Natan as a film extra in Joinville studios. During World War II, he was assistant stage manager on H. G. Clouzot's *Le Corbeau* (1943) at the notorious German-owned Continental Films company.

10. Michel Carré Jr. (1865–1945) was the son of librettist Michel Carré Sr. (1821–1872), who wrote, among other works, the libretti of Gounod's *Faust* and Offenbach's *The Tales of Hoffmann*.

11. SCAGL register, BiFi.

12. Manuscripts department, BnF.

13. *Cinémagazine,* July 1, 1921, 1. Paul Capellani's sculpture is now in the museum at Mont-Saint-Michel.

14. *Moving Picture World,* October 16, 1909, 531.

15. A restaurant combining music and dancing in the outskirts of Paris.

16. *Moving Picture World,* October 16, 1909, 531.

17. Pierre Trimbach, *Quand on tournait la manivelle . . . il y a 60 ans . . . ou les mémoires d'un opérateur de la Belle Epoque* (Paris: CEFAG, 1970), 52.

18. Adrien Vély, "Une tranche de cinéma," *Le Gaulois,* April 5, 1911, 1–2. The film was found by Mariann Lewinsky in Amsterdam (see filmography).

5. *Les Misérables*

1. At 16 fps.
2. *Pathé-Journal,* no. 5, 1912, 15.
3. SCAGL register, BiFi. Mariann Lewinsky notes that *Athalie* was a very bad picture, quite unlike those of Capellani and more like those of Michel Carré, an untalented director.
4. Figures quoted by Richard Abel, *The Ciné Goes to Town: French Cinema, 1896–1914* (Berkeley: University of California Press, 1994), 322.
5. Letter from Gustave Simon to Albert Capellani, June 25, 1912, Maison de Victor Hugo Museum, Paris.
6. Letter from Capellani to Simon, July 1, 1912, Maison de Victor Hugo Museum, Paris.
7. Letter from Simon to Capellani, July 2, 1912, Maison de Victor Hugo Museum, Paris.
8. Letter from Gustave Simon to Madame [Jeanne Hugo?], December 16, 1912, Maison de Victor Hugo Museum, Paris.
9. Commission de Recherche Historique (Historical Research Committee), February 7, 1948, BiFi.
10. Publicity sheet for *Les Misérables,* undated, probably from November–December 1912, Fondation Jérôme Seydoux-Pathé, Paris.
11. *Moving Picture World,* April 5, 1913, 11.
12. *Moving Picture World,* April 26, 1913, 362.
13. *Motion Picture News,* August 4, 1917, 853. In August 1917, a new, eight-reel version of *Les Misérables* was shown again in Chicago.

6. Filmmaker

1. A remake of *La Glu* was filmed in 1927 by Henri Fescourt with Germaine Rouer in the title role. The film was shot in Ouessant Island.
2. *Ciné-Journal,* July 12, 1913.
3. *Moving Picture World,* August 15, 1914, 940.
4. *Le Petit Parisien,* November 7, 1913, 6.
5. *Motion Picture News,* January 31, 1914, 29.
6. *Moving Picture World,* January 24, 1914, 416.

7. End of Reel

1. Pierre Trimbach, *Quand on tournait la manivelle . . . il y a 60 ans . . . ou les mémoires d'un opérateur de la Belle Epoque* (Paris: CEFAG, 1970), 121.
2. Capellani of course is mistaken. It's Gauvain who is guillotined in the film. *Cinémagazine,* April 20, 1923, 112.
3. André-Paul Antoine, *Antoine père et fils* (Paris: R. Julliard, 1962), 206.
4. *Cinémagazine,* February 10, 1921, 5–6.

8. On the Front Line

1. *Moving Picture World,* October 20, 1917, 393.
2. *Photoplay,* January 1917, 90.
3. *Le Petit Parisien,* October 7, 1914, 2.

9. Going or Staying

1. Letter from Léon Gaumont to Louis Feuillade, March 10, 1915, from *Louis Feuillade—retour aux sources* (Paris: AFRHC–Gaumont, 2007), 85.
2. The countess was Marcel Proust's main model for the character of the Duchess of Guermantes in *A la recherche du temps perdu.*
3. Letter from Pierre Decourcelle to André Antoine, December 6, 1914, Antoine papers, BnF.
4. Letter from Decourcelle to Antoine, June 4, 1914, Antoine papers, BnF.
5. Letter from Decourcelle to Antoine, April 9, 1915, Antoine papers, BnF.
6. Letter from Antoine to Decourcelle, February 2, 1916, BnF.
7. Letter from Léon Gaumont to Louis Feuillade, March 10, 1915, from *Louis Feuillade—retour aux sources,* 85.
8. Letter from Feuillade to Gaumont, April 12, 1915, from *Louis Feuillade—retour aux sources,* 90.

10. The Visualizer of *Les Misérables*

1. Unidentified American press clipping, around January or February 1918, Bernard Basset-Capellani Collection.
2. *Moving Picture World,* April 24, 1915, 541.
3. *Photoplay,* July 1915, 55.
4. *Le Film,* August 15, 1919, 28.
5. *Moving Picture World,* June 5, 1915, 1609.
6. *Moving Picture World,* October 2, 1915, 64.

11. World Film Corporation

1. Ben Carré, "Reminiscences of My Years as Motion Picture Art Director" (unpublished manuscript), 180. Kevin Brownlow Collection.
2. The AFI catalog states that the cameraman was played by Josef von Sternberg. If Sternberg was indeed employed as a film cutter at the World Film Corporation at the time, he could not be the person in the film. The man in the movie looks to be extremely short, around 5 feet; Sternberg was considerably taller, around 5 feet 7 inches.
3. *Moving Picture World,* July 3, 1915, 80.
4. *Variety,* July 9, 1915, 18.
5. *Moving Picture World,* September 11, 1915, 1845.
6. *Variety,* October 15, 1915, 21.
7. Frances Marion, *Off With Their Heads! A Serio-Comic Tale of Hollywood* (New York: Macmillan, 1972), 33.
8. Ibid., 32–33.
9. Ibid., 35.
10. *Moving Picture World,* December 18, 1915, 2161.
11. *Moving Picture World,* November 6, 1915, 1159.
12. *Photoplay,* March 1916, 109.
13. Bernard Basset-Capellani Collection.
14. *Moving Picture World,* January 8, 1916, 253.
15. *Variety,* January 7, 1916, 23.
16. *Variety,* January 28, 1916, 28.
17. *Motion Picture News,* May 13, 1916, 2912.
18. *Variety,* April 28, 1916, 29.
19. *Moving Picture World,* May 13, 1916, 1176.

20. Albert Capellani, his brother Paul, and cameraman Lucien Andriot returned from Havana on February 19, 1916.

21. *Variety*, July 7, 1916, 22.

22. Interview with Paul Capellani in *Cinémagazine*, July 1, 1921, 3; fan letter from the Bernard Basset-Capellani Collection.

23. *Moving Picture World*, July 1, 1916, 100.

24. *Variety*, June 16, 1916, 24.

25. *Moving Picture World*, September 30, 1916, 2096.

12. Woman's Director

1. Frances Marion, *Off With Their Heads! A Serio-Comic Tale of Hollywood* (New York: Macmillan, 1972), 35.

2. *Variety*, July 7, 1916, 22.

3. Marion, *Off With Their Heads*, 34.

4. *Moving Picture World*, July 15, 1916, 466.

5. Henry Bernstein's *Le Voleur* was produced in 1906. It created a stir at the time with its forty-five-minute second act containing only two characters. Maurice Tourneur adapted Bernstein's play to the screen in 1933 with Madeleine Renaud and Victor Francen.

6. *Moving Picture World*, July 15, 1916, 466.

7. Ibid.

8. Capellani may have subscribed to such a precept, but we must remember that the sign was observed at the Solax studio—a studio created by Alice Guy-Blaché. Guy-Blaché claimed to have been the first person to devise such an exhortation, though we have to take her word for it.

9. *Photoplay*, January 1917, 88.

10. In 1916–1917, Josef von Sternberg—then called Joe Stern— was working at World. His mentor was Emile Chautard.

11. *Photoplay*, January 1917, 89–90. The technique employed by Capellani to direct his actors was taken up by Clarence Brown, who was then Maurice Tourneur's assistant.

12. Ben Carré, "Reminiscences of My Years as Motion Picture Art Director" (unpublished manuscript), 181. Kevin Brownlow Collection.

13. *Motion Picture News*, August 19, 1916, 1067.

14. *Moving Picture World,* October 7, 1916, 65.

15. *Variety,* September 29, 1916, 24.

16. *Photoplay,* December 1916, 81.

17. *Photoplay,* January 1917, 89.

18. Lenore Coffee, *Storyline: Recollections of a Hollywood Screenwriter* (London: Cassell, 1973), 39.

19. *Photoplay,* December 1916, 81.

20. The style and misspellings suggest the author of this letter may have been of German origin. Bernard Basset-Capellani Collection.

21. *Photoplay,* March 1917, 120.

22. *Moving Picture World,* December 30, 1916, 1975.

23. *Moving Picture World,* May 26, 1917, 1317.

24. The film was 110 minutes long.

25. *Variety,* April 13, 1917, 26.

26. *Moving Picture World,* April 28, 1917, 635.

27. Unidentified American press clipping, around January or February 1918. Bernard Basset-Capellani Collection.

28. Marion, *Off With Their Heads,* 35.

13. Transition at Mutual

1. *Moving Picture World,* June 23, 1917, 1946.

2. *Motion Picture News,* July 14, 1917, 173.

3. Dell Henderson was also an actor. He played Marion Davies's father in two King Vidor comedies, *The Patsy* (1928) and *Show People* (1928).

4. *Variety,* December 7, 1917, 50.

5. *Moving Picture World,* October 20, 1917, 393.

6. *Moving Picture World,* October 27, 1917, 530.

7. *Cine Mundial,* June 1918, 332.

8. *Film Daily,* December 16, 1918, 2.

9. *Ciné Pour Tous,* June 5, 1920, 2.

10. I recently wrote a biography of Maurice Tourneur, which uncovers the details surrounding these events: *Maurice Tourneur: Réalisateur sans frontières* (Grandvilliers: La Tour Verte, 2015).

11. Letter from Paul Capellani to André Antoine, May 12, 1919, André Antoine papers, BnF.

14. Metro Director

1. *Variety,* January 11, 1918, 46.
2. *Variety,* April 12, 1918, 42.
3. Actress Katherine Corri Harris (1890–1927) was John Barry-more's first wife.
4. *Variety,* August 16, 1918, 38.
5. *Moving Picture World,* August 24, 1918, 1154.
6. *Film Daily,* August 10, 1918, 4.
7. *Moving Picture World,* June 1, 1918, 1308.
8. *Moving Picture World,* September 14, 1918, 1568. The play was later adapted for the screen by Henri Fescourt in France in 1927 under the title *L'Occident,* with the hilariously untalented Claudia Victrix playing the Nazimova part.
9. Charles Bryant was Nazimova's companion—though she introduced him as her husband. He also directed several of her films.
10. *Variety,* November 22, 1918, 44.
11. *Film Daily,* December 27, 1918, 4.
12. Henri Ménessier interview, 1946–1948, Commission de Recherche Historique (Historical Research Committee), BiFi.
13. *Film Daily,* February 6, 1919, 3.
14. *Variety,* February 21, 1919, 68.
15. *Film Daily,* March 4, 1919, 1.
16. *Children of Eve* (1915) was released on DVD in the United States with *Devil's Needle* by Kino Video. Three reels of *Flower of the Dusk* (1918) have been preserved by the Archives françaises du film in Bois d'Arcy.

15. *The Red Lantern*

1. The film was released on DVD by the Cinémathèque Royale de Belgique.
2. *Moving Picture World,* January 4, 1919, 103. The author of this article misspells his name as "Jim Wong" instead of Wang. James Wang was often used as talent scout for pictures in need of Chinese extras. See Kevin Brownlow, *Behind the Mask of Innocence* (London: Jonathan Cape, 1990), 332.
3. *Film Daily,* April 23, 1919, 2.

4. *Le Film,* August 19, 1919, 28.
5. *Moving Picture World,* January 25, 1919, 512.
6. *Cinémagazine,* May 20, 1921, 10.
7. Jack Spears, *The Civil War on the Screen and Other Essays* (South Brunswick, NJ: A. S. Barnes, 1977), 132.
8. *Moving Picture World,* January 25, 1919, 475.
9. *Motion Picture News,* May 10, 1919, 3061.
10. *Cinémagazine,* April 20, 1923, 114.
11. *Variety,* May 9, 1919, 53.
12. *Moving Picture World,* May 10, 1919, 933.
13. Gavin Lambert, *Nazimova: A Biography* (New York: Alfred A. Knopf, 1997), 213.
14. *Photoplay,* May 1919, 88.

16. Albert Capellani Productions, Inc.

1. *Film Daily,* February 23, 1919, 3.
2. *Moving Picture World,* March 8, 1919, 1345.
3. *Film Daily,* March 11, 1919; March 12, 1919; March 27, 1919; April 24, 1919; May 5, 1919.
4. *Variety,* June 13, 1919, 49.
5. *Film Daily,* June 12, 1919, 3.
6. Lucien Tainguy was the cameraman. *Variety,* August 8, 1919, 49.
7. *Variety,* October 17, 1919, 63.
8. *Variety,* September 19, 1919, 54.
9. *Moving Picture World,* September 27, 1919, 2024.
10. *Le Film,* August 15, 1919, 30.
11. *Film Daily,* December 7, 1919, 18.
12. *Film Daily,* December 22, 1919, 1.
13. *New York Times,* December 21, 1919, 20.
14. *Film Daily,* January 16, 1920, 1.
15. *Variety,* May 14, 1920, 34.
16. *Moving Picture World,* May 22, 1920, 1107.

17. Cosmopolitan Productions

1. *Variety,* January 14, 1921, 41.
2. *Moving Picture World,* January 22, 1921, 465.

3. *Film Daily,* August 28, 1920, 2.

4. *Film Daily,* September 28, 1920, 4.

5. *Film Daily,* October 1, 1920, 2.

6. *Motion Picture News,* undated press clipping probably circa April 1921. Bernard Basset-Capellani Collection.

7. Ibid.

8. *Film Daily,* April 21, 1921, 3.

9. *Film Daily,* June 8, 1922, 2; *Variety,* June 16, 1922, 21.

10. *Moving Picture World,* May 21, 1921, 327.

11. Ibid.

12. Unidentified press clipping, June 27, 1921, Rondel papers, BnF.

13. Unidentified press clipping, July 5, 1921, Rondel papers, BnF.

14. *Cinémagazine,* June 24, 1921, 26.

15. *Variety,* May 13, 1921, 42.

16. *Film Daily,* May 15, 1921, 7.

17. *Variety,* April 7, 1922, 41.

18. *Film Daily,* April 9, 1922, 5.

19. *Variety,* September 1, 1922, 41.

20. *Film Daily,* July 30, 1922, 9.

21. Ben Carré, "Reminiscences of My Years as Motion Picture Art Director" (unpublished manuscript), 182. Kevin Brownlow Collection.

18. Back Home

1. *Cinémagazine,* April 20, 1923, 114.

2. Letter from Mr. Dauny to Mr. Pouchet, July 8, 1923, Serge Sandberg papers, BnF.

3. *Cinéa-Ciné Pour Tous,* September 1, 1927, 32.

4. *Cinémonde,* December 26, 1929, 1082.

5. *Cinéopse,* no. 147, November 1931.

6. Kristin Thompson, *David Bordwell's Website on Cinema—Observations on Film Art,* blog, July 14, 2011, http://www.davidbordwell .net/blog/2011/07/14/capellani-trionfante/.

Filmography

1. All French films are Pathé productions. This filmography was based on the Pathé catalogs established by Henri Bousquet (as well as

the updated online catalog from the Fondation Jérôme Sedoux-Pathé), supplemented by notes on new films that were added following recent discoveries. Some films were removed from Bousquet's list when new sources provided information disproving the attribution to Capellani.

2. Capellani is identified as director by Hughes Laurent, "Souvenirs de 50 ans ! . . . " in *Bulletin de l'Association Française des Ingénieurs et Techniciens du cinéma,* 1957, no. 16, 8.

3. According to Mariann Lewinsky, the picture looks visually like a Capellani. But no sources can confirm it.

4. Film mentioned in the SCAGL register (BiFi), but the title could not be identified in the Pathé catalog.

5. Henri Bousquet attributes the film to Georges Denola. But the A. Boudier register of correspondence (Georges Sadoul papers, BiFi) shows it's a Capellani.

6. Henri Bousquet's catalog indicates erroneously that Albert Dieudonné (then aged twenty-two) played the part of Old Lesurques. In fact, it's his uncle, Alphonse Dieudonné (I viewed the BFI print). Besides, Albert Dieudonné didn't start making films until 1915 (source: Kevin Brownlow).

7. Director identified thanks to an article from *Le Gaulois,* April 5, 1911, where screenwriter Adrien Vély mentions Capellani as director. Complete print identified by Mariann Lewinsky. Dutch title: *Paris het modern Babylon.*

8. Film attributed to Michel Carré by H. Bousquet. But the A. Boudier register of correspondence (Sadoul papers, BiFi) shows it's Capellani who made it. This is confirmed by Pierre Trimbach's memoirs.

9. According to the A. Boudier register of correspondence (Sadoul papers, BiFi).

10. According to the A. Boudier register of correspondence (Sadoul papers, BiFi). Title and release date not identified.

11. Henri Bousquet attributes the film to Georges Denola. But according to Pierre Trimbach's memoirs, Capellani directed it.

12. According to Mariann Lewinsky, the picture looks visually like a Capellani. But no sources can confirm it.

13. According to Pierre Trimbach, Le Forestier directed it under Capellani's supervision.

14. According to the A. Boudier register of correspondence (Sadoul papers, BiFi).

15. According to the A. Boudier register of correspondence (Sadoul papers, BiFi).

16. The American filmography is based upon the American Film Institute Catalog.

17. Ben Carré mentions in his unpublished memoirs having worked on this film as well as on *La Vie de Bohème*. He also mentions working on other Capellani productions, but couldn't remember the titles.

Selected Bibliography

Abel, Richard. *The Ciné Goes to Town: French Cinema, 1896–1914.* Berkeley: University of California Press, 1994.

Antoine, André. *Mes souvenirs sur le théâtre Antoine et l'Odéon.* Paris: Grasset, 1928.

Antoine, André-Paul. *Antoine père et fils.* Paris: R. Julliard, 1962.

Blum, Daniel. *A Pictorial History of the Silent Screen.* New York: Grosset & Dunlap, 1953.

Bodeen, DeWitt. *More from Hollywood: The Career of Fifteen Great American Stars.* South Brunswick, NJ: A. S. Barnes/Tantivy Press, 1977.

Bousquet, Henri. *Catalogue Pathé des années 1896–1914.* 4 vols. Bures-sur-Yvette: H. Bousquet, 1993–1996.

Brownlow, Kevin. *Behind the Mask of Innocence.* London: Jonathan Cape, 1990.

———. *The Parade's Gone By. . . .* Berkeley: University of California Press, 1968.

Carou, Alain. *Le cinéma français et les écrivains: Histoire d'une rencontre, 1906–1914.* Paris: Ecole Nationale des Chartes/AFHRC, 2002.

Coffee, Lenore. *Storyline: Recollections of a Hollywood Screenwriter.* London: Cassell, 1973.

Dixon, Bryony. *100 Silent Films.* London: BFI/Palgrave Macmillan, 2011.

Guy, Alice. *Autobiographie d'une pionnière du cinéma (1873–1968).* Paris: Denoël/Gonthier, 1976.

Haver, Ronald. *David O. Selznick's Hollywood.* New York: Bonanza Books, 1980.

Kermabon, Jacques, ed. *Pathé: Premier empire du cinéma.* Paris: Centre Georges Pompidou, 1994.

Koszarski, Richard. *Fort Lee—The Film Town.* Rome: John Libbey Publishing, 2004.

Marion, Frances. *Off With Their Heads! A Serio-Comic Tale of Hollywood.* New York: Macmillan, 1972.

Ramsaye, Terry. *A Million and One Nights: A History of the Motion Picture through 1925.* New York: Touchstone Books, 1986.

Spears, Jack. *The Civil War on the Screen and Other Essays.* South Brunswick, NJ: A. S. Barnes, 1977.

Tattersall, Robert. *Diabetes: The Biography.* Oxford: Oxford University Press, 2009.

Trimbach, Pierre. *Quand on tournait la manivelle . . . il y a 60 ans . . . ou les mémoires d'un opérateur de la Belle Epoque.* Paris: CEFAG, 1970.

Index

Index

Index

Index

Screen Classics

Screen Classics is a series of critical biographies, film histories, and analytical studies focusing on neglected filmmakers and important screen artists and subjects, from the era of silent cinema to the golden age of Hollywood to the international generation of today. Books in the Screen Classics series are intended for scholars and general readers alike. The contributing authors are established figures in their respective fields. This series also serves the purpose of advancing scholarship on film personalities and themes with ties to Kentucky.

Series Editor

Patrick McGilligan

Books in the Series

Mae Murray: The Girl with the Bee-Stung Lips
  Michael G. Ankerich
Hedy Lamarr: The Most Beautiful Woman in Film
  Ruth Barton
Rex Ingram: Visionary Director of the Silent Screen
  Ruth Barton
Von Sternberg
  John Baxter
Hitchcock's Partner in Suspense: The Life of Screenwriter Charles Bennett
  Charles Bennett, edited by John Charles Bennett
Ziegfeld and His Follies: A Biography of Broadway's Greatest Producer
  Cynthia Brideson and Sara Brideson
The Marxist and the Movies: A Biography of Paul Jarrico
  Larry Ceplair
Dalton Trumbo: Blacklisted Hollywood Radical
  Larry Ceplair and Christopher Trumbo
Warren Oates: A Wild Life
  Susan Compo
Crane: Sex, Celebrity, and My Father's Unsolved Murder
  Robert Crane and Christopher Fryer
Jack Nicholson: The Early Years
  Robert Crane and Christopher Fryer
Being Hal Ashby: Life of a Hollywood Rebel
  Nick Dawson
Bruce Dern: A Memoir
  Bruce Dern with Christopher Fryer and Robert Crane
Intrepid Laughter: Preston Sturges and the Movies
  Andrew Dickos
John Gilbert: The Last of the Silent Film Stars
  Eve Golden

Stuntwomen: The Untold Hollywood Story
  Mollie Gregory
Saul Bass: Anatomy of Film Design
  Jan-Christopher Horak
Hitchcock Lost and Found: The Forgotten Films
  Alain Kerzoncuf and Charles Barr
Pola Negri: Hollywood's First Femme Fatale
  Mariusz Kotowski
Sidney J. Furie: Life and Films
  Daniel Kremer
Albert Capellani: Pioneer of the Silent Screen
  Christine Leteux
Mamoulian: Life on Stage and Screen
  David Luhrssen
Maureen O'Hara: The Biography
  Aubrey Malone
My Life as a Mankiewicz: An Insider's Journey through Hollywood
  Tom Mankiewicz and Robert Crane
Hawks on Hawks
  Joseph McBride
William Wyler: The Life and Films of Hollywood's Most Celebrated Director
  Gabriel Miller
Raoul Walsh: The True Adventures of Hollywood's Legendary Director
  Marilyn Ann Moss
Charles Walters: The Director Who Made Hollywood Dance
  Brent Phillips
Some Like It Wilder: The Life and Controversial Films of Billy Wilder
  Gene D. Phillips
Ann Dvorak: Hollywood's Forgotten Rebel
  Christina Rice
Arthur Penn: American Director
  Nat Segaloff
Claude Rains: An Actor's Voice
  David J. Skal with Jessica Rains
Buzz: The Life and Art of Busby Berkeley
  Jeffrey Spivak
Victor Fleming: An American Movie Master
  Michael Sragow
Hollywood Presents Jules Verne: The Father of Science Fiction on Screen
  Brian Taves
Thomas Ince: Hollywood's Independent Pioneer
  Brian Taves
Carl Theodor Dreyer and Ordet: *My Summer with the Danish Filmmaker*
  Jan Wahl

www.ingramcontent.com/pod-product-compliance
Lightning Source LLC
Chambersburg PA
CBHW020452100426
42813CB00031B/3337/J